HISTORIC
OXFORD

Oxford has always been a bookish place. One day in 1953 Dr Claude Jenkins (1877-1959), Regius Professor of Ecclesiastical History from 1934, limped in a bit late to give a lecture in the Chapter House. As he went out my brother and his two or three other students crowded round to ask if he was all right; he assured them that it was 'just a fall of books on the stairs'. His lodgings were the middle of the east range of Tom Quad. I remember him in 1958, glancing round from the pulpit to check that the dean was listening, before he began to preach: 'Being of a modest but *not* a retiring disposition….' 'Canon Claude' spent his vacations in his bookshop at Tunbridge Wells, leaving his lodgings, as seen here, crammed with books

HISTORIC
OXFORD

DAVID STURDY

TEMPUS

For Argo
Steadfast companion for 18 years
7 September 1985 – 3 February 2004

First published 2004

Tempus Publishing Ltd
The Mill, Brimscombe Port
Stroud, Gloucestershire GL5 2QG
www.tempus-publishing.com

British Library Cataloguing in Publication Data.
A catalogue record for this book is available from the British Library.

ISBN 0 7524 3150 1

Typesetting and origination by Tempus Publishing.
Printed and bound in Great Britain.

CONTENTS

1 The town seal of an Ox, twelfth century

INTRODUCTION
CITIES, FORDS & MYTHS

In the twelfth century the leading citizens of Oxford chose a communal seal showing a city of towers defended by battlements with, in the foreground, the bold and protective Ox which gave the place its name (*1*). None of the countless boundary stones and cast-iron lamp-posts throughout the city, or any of the coats of arms and recent 'logos', shows the Ox harnessed or pulling a plough or a cart. To all proper citizens the Ox is a protective totem or emblem, fit to be painted on fire-buckets or battle-standards, as it was in Tudor and Stuart times. To outsiders our Ox should be fierce and wild, not a tame beast. In 1588 the city militia marched east for 140km to Essex, to face battle-hardened Spanish troops from Holland (if the Armada had got them across the Channel) with the city's Ox fluttering above them. The banner carried on this occasion was treasured; the city council voted a reward of 40 shillings to Captain Warde 'in consideracion that he brought the colours of this Citie safelye backe fromme Tilberie'.

The precise location of the ford which gave its name to the city is documented in a property deed of 1352 about a narrow plot of meadow, naming the 'Ox-Ford', 1,500m west of the central crossroads at Carfax and 500m south of the main route west from the city, the Botley Road. Two pioneer local historians, Brian Twyne (1579-1644) and Anthony Wood (1632-95), knew and understood the deed. Superseded for everyday use by a steel footbridge (*colour plate 1*), the 'Ox-Ford' lies at a most interesting spot on a Roman road from the south-west, which stops there and has been traced no further to the north-east, although it may one day be found in the grounds of Worcester College. Just downstream from the ford the Minster Ditch, dredged in the 1890s, produced some memorable finds, including an axe and a spearhead of the Bronze Age, an iron dagger in an ornate bronze sheath and a brooch, both of Iron Age date, and two Anglo-Saxon iron spearheads (*colour plate 3*). In 1889 Andrew Clark, an industrious local clergyman, edited Wood's *City of Oxford* and got confused about the deed of 1352; his footnote locates the ford on 'one of the streams which runs between Botley and Oxford Castle', meaning on the Botley Road. In 1917 H.E. Salter, an even more scholarly and industrious clergyman, published a reference to the ford in papers of a lawsuit of 1376 between the town and Oseney Abbey about boundaries and jurisdictions, but could not place it exactly. Later, while preparing college archives for publication, Salter came across the original deed of 1352 and was able to locate the ford with the help of a map made in 1848 when the meadows were enclosed. He wrote a short article, 'The Ford of Oxford', and sent it to a new journal, *Antiquity*, founded by O.G.S. Crawford, geographer, air photographer and archaeology officer at the Ordnance Survey, who published it in 1928. In 1929 Salter published the deed in full with hundreds of others. Six years later, in a lecture in 1935, he pointed out that 'This is not a new discovery. Anthony Wood noted the former passage (of 1352)'. Certainty, as so often at Oxford, has been followed by wilful confusion. In the last 30 years some people have been deluded into supposing that the *real* 'Oxenford' ran along the line of St Aldate's, south from Carfax (*9b*), and archaeologists have wasted much time and energy 'proving' this fallacy. In 1973 the late Professor R.H.C. Davis, who often meddled in things he knew nothing about, wrote an article asserting that the St Aldate's line was 'the original oxen's ford', consisting of 'a whole series of fords which could be negotiated by heavy ox-carts', and claimed that the citizens' case in 1376 was a fraudulent attempt to extend their jurisdiction. He ignored three vital bits of evidence: the Roman Road, the finds from the Minster Ditch, and the earlier deed of 1352 which showed where the ford was. He also failed to explain that the lawsuit was just one of many boundary disputes in the fourteenth century, when the town was in slow decay, and in the seventeenth, when the city was rapidly expanding.

If we lacked the vital evidence of 1352 there are many fords all round Oxford, any or all of which might be *the* ford. It is worth adding that the name of the channel upstream from the 'Ox-ford' is the Bulstake Stream, which rather suggests that there was a post on the stream carved with a bull or a bull's head, or even perhaps a bull's skull nailed to a post (p.127). The 'Ox-ford' may have been a place of sacrifice or of a reputed or legendary battle; at some date the skeleton of a wild ox, an aurochs or *Bos primigenius*, may have been found there in old river silts or Pleistocene gravel deposits; or there may have been a battle there in late Saxon times, perhaps in the reign of King Alfred, when warriors fighting under a banner of a wild ox triumphed, whether over other English warriors or over a group of Vikings. After all, another river crossing named for an animal, Pegasus Bridge in Normandy, bears the name of the legendary winged horse and symbol of poetry that was worn as a shoulder badge by our local regiment, the Oxfordshire and Buckinghamshire Light Infantry, when they led the invasion on D-Day in 1944. It is pedestrian and unimaginative to suppose that the name Oxford is about 'heavy ox-carts' crossing 'a whole series of fords'.

Oxford's chief gift to civilisation is the place itself, rather than any branch of knowledge. It is a fascinating, beautiful, infuriating, overcrowded city, easy to get acquainted with in a superficial way, impossible to understand thoroughly.

Many mysterious tales have been told about the town and strange legends concocted about the university. Oxford's origin was the subject of much speculation and discussion in the centuries when the identity of the ford was forgotten or half-lost. Nominally a place of learning, the city is full of myth, legend, fantasy, notions, memories, reputations, ghosts. A walk through the historic centre of the city and university should be one of the world's great visual and architectural experiences. Unless we are very lucky, the pleasure got from looking about us as we wander round the streets will be ruined by buses, vans, shoppers, tourists, students, intrusive hangers-on attracted by the city's air of success and culture of greed. And yet to understand the place we must see it and walk round it repeatedly – live there for a time if we can. I lived in Oxford for 40 years, in 1939-66 and 1983-93, and now live a short train-ride away. I can never forget the day we came to Oxford, in September 1939, the week before the Second World War broke out. My father's Singer was the only car parked in a very wide street – St Giles as I later found out – as we sat in a tearoom, bathed in glittering late-summer sunshine. That morning we had left my birthplace, a black Yorkshire valley, a city of steel and industrial smog, Victorian technology tooling up for re-armament half a century after that industry's prime. By a miracle the public telephone service, the GPO, needed an electronic engineer at short notice and posted my father south from Sheffield to Oxford. It was a kind of paradise and remains the most beautiful city I have ever seen, except on a dull grey overcrowded day. I used to bicycle to school in Brewer Street and later Cowley Place, or pay a penny-halfpenny child's fare on the No.5 bus. I walked endlessly round, in and out of every church and college. There were no barriers or restrictions. For the next six years there were no tourists, almost no students and few shoppers. Many deliveries still went by horse and cart. As a mere schoolboy I would lift my cap as an academic dignitary went past, preceded by his bedell with a silver staff, and marvel that the vice-chancellor, in full academicals, would graciously doff his mortarboard to me. I never wondered, as I do now, how the place came to be as it was.

More than most cities, Oxford is a theatre, its scenery all standing, the actors taking their parts without being aware of it, or only half aware, as dreams and fantasy are all around. The whole place is a spectacular and unforgettable advertisement for education, for young people to meet each other, talk to their elders, and discover how to get on in real life. Every corner of the city has links with other parts of the country – often with other parts of the world. We can wonder how the place has contrived to make a decent living in this way for eight centuries, while dominating many aspects of national life: government service, the Church, the law, diplomacy, politics, far more than her younger sister Cambridge, which produced scientists and poets. Oxford has always greedily sought change. In the nineteenth century she took an interest in the Empire, especially India. In the twentieth century she turned her interest to America and international affairs. Within the main theatre that is the city there are many lesser ones. Clustered tightly together behind the main shopping streets, there are 20 or 21 ancient colleges, all well worth visiting if they happen to be open that day and you can find the way in. They are all private, hidden behind high stone walls but often quite welcoming once you find the way. Enclosed courtyards or 'quads' linked by passages contain a chapel, a dining hall, a library, offices, common rooms and residential ranges planned and built in 'staircases'. The beauty is all around, elusive and often well hidden, but never averse to giving us a glance of secret charms behind locked gates. As if to deny how hard it is to get to know them better, some colleges have quite grand, almost showy façades, none pompous or over life-size. At centre stage as an essential part of the show among the colleges, the university's own six most historic buildings, modestly grand, intriguing and striking, stand in or near Radcliffe Square. Built between the 1270s and the 1740s, they are in use every day, sometimes for more or less their original purpose. The earliest is still by far the tallest building in the city, one of Oxford's great mysteries. Who thought up St Mary's tower in about 1270 and had the initiative to raise the funds? And who else continued the momentum to complete the spire by about 1325? Next to it, the most recent of the six buildings is a great round library; its fabulous dome always provides intense visual satisfaction at any time of day or night. We know a fair amount about the benefactor, John Radcliffe (1652–1713), a poor boy from Yorkshire who studied at Oxford, became a fashionable London doctor and left a fortune. In the 1730s and '40s, with several changes of plan, his trustees, their architects and builders created this magnificent rotunda, which he never knew.

Every city or town is its own best guide, to be walked round and enjoyed by looking and examining. This is especially true of Oxford; we should walk until our feet ache, exploring the streets, houses, churches, colleges and other buildings, then sit in a shady spot to ponder and glance at a map or book. In most towns and cities local libraries and archives contain old drawings and photographs, both of what we can see, and of buildings that have been torn down, burnt, blown up or bombed; but Oxford was never bombed. Local museums have other records and artefacts, as well as fragments of lost houses and churches. This book will concentrate on the architecture and archaeology of Oxford, remains that can be seen every day, referring sometimes to records. It will say less about the medieval colleges and more about Cornmarket, the crowded main shopping street, and its large, visually dreary, modern stores. Residents and visitors can easily learn something of the colleges and their rich history and fine buildings. It is much harder for them to grasp and understand what was learnt about the city's past when the stores were built in the 1950s and '60s. I was involved and can write about it at first hand. For centuries archaeological discoveries have been recorded, if not always understood, and will continue to be found, if not fully understood, for centuries more.

2 St Aldate's, with Lewis Carroll's rooms at Christ Church, on the site of Wolsey's chapel (*60*) in the 1520s, of London College in the 1410s, Burnells Inn in the 1290s and the earlier synagogue. Taunt, *Oxford Illustrated by Camera and Pen* (1911)

Oxford has layer upon layer of memories, history, archaeology, architecture, countless records and ancient documents, drawings, prints and photographs of every part of the city. The evidence, the events and the buildings crowd together and succeed each other closely. At one point, between the Head Post Office in St Aldate's and Pembroke Street, we can look across the street at the splendid octagonal north towers of Christ Church (*2*) where, in his rooms on the upper floor, the mathematician C.L. Dodgson (Lewis Carroll) wrote *Alice in Wonderland* in the 1860s. This part of the college was built in the 1660s by John Fell, dean of Christ Church. He, or his father, demolished the walls of a vast chapel left unfinished by the great statesman Thomas Wolsey, archbishop of York and chancellor of England when he fell from power in 1529 (p.125). A century earlier Richard Clifford, bishop of London, had started to establish a smaller college on this site where, still earlier, the princely chancellor of England and bishop of Bath and Wells, Robert Burnell, and his brother William had begun to found a college in the 1290s. Their site, the synagogue and some adjoining houses, came on the market when the Jews were expelled in 1290. Nothing of the synagogue or of Burnells Inn remains above ground, but we can admire Burnell's battlemented manor house at his old family estate, Acton Burnell in Shropshire, 200km north-west of Oxford, and his great hall and chapel at the Bishop's Palace at Wells, 150km to the south-west. Wolsey seems to speak to us every day from Whitehall, his London palace and our seat of government since Henry VIII seized it; much remains of his palace at Hampton

Court which Henry also took. Europe has marvellous churches, castles, and town walls, but we always want to know more about the houses and lesser institutions, their patrons, owners and builders, whose records are not always easy to find. Some towns in France, Italy and Croatia have dozens of medieval houses and almshouses. So do a few English towns like Weobley in Herefordshire, Lavenham in Suffolk, or Burford in Oxfordshire. With no more than a dozen medieval houses, all much altered, Oxford is not the place to study medieval domestic architecture; in any case most of the houses were not family homes, but inns or student hostels. Although a wonderful location to study change and continuity over 1,000 years and more, Oxford cannot compare for antiquity with the cities of London to the east, Winchester to the south, Gloucester to the west, or Leicester to the north. They stand above the remains of Roman towns, although they cannot claim much continuity of urban life through Saxon times, having been largely abandoned between the fifth and ninth centuries AD. Locally Oxford is not as ancient as the small town of Abingdon which has buried beneath it a Roman town and, below that, a great Iron Age fortress, with Bronze Age barrows nearby as well as a Neolithic 'causewayed camp'. Abingdon claims to have been inhabited for thousands of years.

We should note in a world context that most great cities began as trading posts, mission stations or forts. New York (New Amsterdam 1611-24; captured and renamed 1664) and Southampton (Hamwic by 840) were trading posts. Munich (ninth century) and Montreal (1642) were mission stations. St Petersburg (1703) and Pittsburgh (Fort Duquesne 1750; Fort Pitt 1758) were forts. Other origins are also attested: one or two cities were government centres almost from the start, like St Petersburg (1703, just after the fort), Canberra (1900-27) or Brasilia (1960). Others, rarely, like Caernarfon (1283) and Philadelphia (1683), were founded as towns and local capitals, with a governor, merchants and artisans. Many cities have several simultaneous or successive origins and, tactfully forgotten, gaps in continuity. In Upper California the first European settlement involved soldiers and friars working hand-in-hand to dominate the local people. San Diego was colonised in 1769, but five years later the friars moved their mission from the fort to an area more suitable for large-scale farming, and then everyone moved away. The modern city, laid out on a new site in the 1860s, has no continuity with either fort or mission. Other cities like San Francisco and Los Angeles have similar complex early histories, the latter with a native village as the first focus. Every city or town has its own myth, often wide of the truth. At Oxford myths multiply so wildly that all three main origins have been claimed and given vocal support.

Turning back to local detail, we find that archaeological finds from within the boundaries of the modern city of Oxford include a few palaeolithic hand-axes, modest quantities of struck flints of neolithic or Bronze Age date, a number of Bronze Age ring-ditches, some Iron Age and Roman farmsteads, enough to show that the area has attracted settlers and farmers in

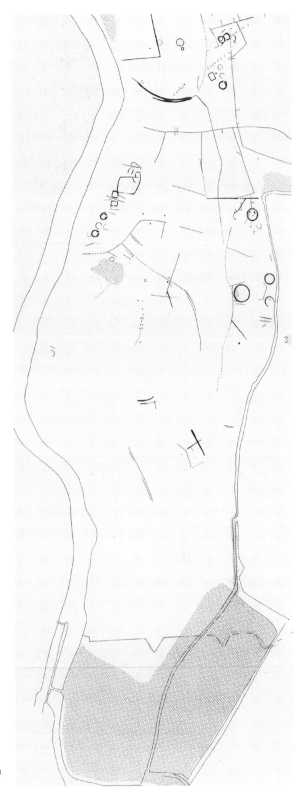

3 Port Meadow, plan of
prehistoric and Roman sites, with
siegework of 1646

4 Binsey: prehistoric and Roman sites as cropmarks, medieval arable fields as 'ridge and furrow', with the Thames on the right. *Aerial photo by G.W.G. Allen, 1933*

modest numbers over the ages (*3, 4; colour plate 3*). Oxford lies between two major prehistoric ritual centres attested by finds, aerial photographs and excavations, one at Eynsham and Stanton Harcourt, 10km west of Oxford, the other at Dorchester-on-Thames, 15km to the south-east. As the local capital during the Iron Age, the Eynsham was succeeded by a great river-fort at Cassington nearby, while the Dorchester sites were succeeded by the hillfort at Wittenham Clumps, then by the river-fort at Dyke Hills, and then by the small Roman town of Dorchester, where St Birinus established a bishopric in the 640s. By contrast the Eynsham area may have declined in importance during and after the Iron Age, and lacks a Roman town as potential local capital. Nearer Oxford there is no sign of any Iron Age fort or Roman town which could have served as a local centre, unlike Abingdon, where the river-fort and Roman town suggest that it may have rivalled Dorchester for several centuries. Thomas Hearne, an acute antiquary of St Edmund Hall, observed in 1709 that:

> There being no Roman coyns found at Oxford, & there being no mention of it in the ancient Itineraries, it seems that 'twas not a place of note in the times of the Romans.

It took a long time for this sensible comment to sink in. Soon after, in 1712, Hearne recorded the finding of a Roman coin 'as they were digging a Cellar' at Carfax (*27a*), without allowing this single find to change his general conclusion. He also wrote about Roman finds from the University Parks and a possible Roman road:

> I have however been told of Coyns that have been found in New-Parks, across wch one Branch of the Roman Ikenild Way pass'd and so went by Witney, where also there have been Coyns of the Romans discover'd lately.

In the mid-1880s James Parker agreed that 'there are no traces of any presence of the Romans during the period of the Roman invasion, in what may be called the immediate vicinity; nor yet of the period of the Roman occupation, though of the latter there are very many traces at some distance from Oxford, and in every direction'. Indeed at least three Roman roads run nearby, one of them narrowly avoiding the medieval town. The first road, Akeman Street, 14km north of Oxford, was a main road linking the second largest city of Roman Britain, Cirencester (Corinium) to the west, with the third largest, St Albans (Verulamium) to the east. The second road, known as Blackberry Lane in its middle section, runs through the outer suburbs of Oxford 4km east of the city centre, a less important route between two small Roman towns,

5 The Thames flood-plain, looking over Port Meadow 'From a cow-shed, in the rain, on the road to Binsey', drawn by J.W. Burgon, vicar of St Mary's, 21 June 1847

6 Bronze Age ring-ditch at University College, with Fr Fabian Radcliffe OP at his dig on
the site of the Goodhart Quadrangle, 1960

Alchester to the north and Dorchester-on-Thames to the south. In the 1840s
Robert Hussey, classics tutor at Christ Church, later first professor of ecclesiastical history, published a description of this road based on his own fieldwork.
Since then many Roman pottery kilns, a large-scale industry, have been found
in that area. A third road, long presumed to be Roman but never confirmed
by excavation, can be traced for 18km between Grove near Wantage and the
outskirts of Oxford (7). This road, something of a 'flying Dutchman' in that it
does not link two Roman towns, does however bring us to the 'Ox-Ford'.
The modern main road past Grove, the A338, runs straight for 6km to the
north-north-east until it crosses the River Ock at the former Noah's Ark Inn,
a Roman temple site of some importance. This stretch, marked 'ROMAN
ROAD' on the latest Ordnance Survey Landranger map (1:50,000 scale) points
towards the Roman town of Alchester to the north-east. The A338, still pretty straight, now turns slightly northward for 5km through Frilford to
Besselsleigh. After a gap a straight alignment of footpaths and hedgerows, on
the same general line, becomes Harcourt Hill, leading past Westminster
College and the outer suburban houses of Oxford to North Hinksey. Here, at
the Fishes public house, we come down on the broad flood-plain, where the
Thames flows in seven or eight channels, man-made, natural or partly natural.
To the north the flood-plain widens but has fewer channels, and to the south
it narrows to the 'Sandford gap' where the Thames flows in a single stream.

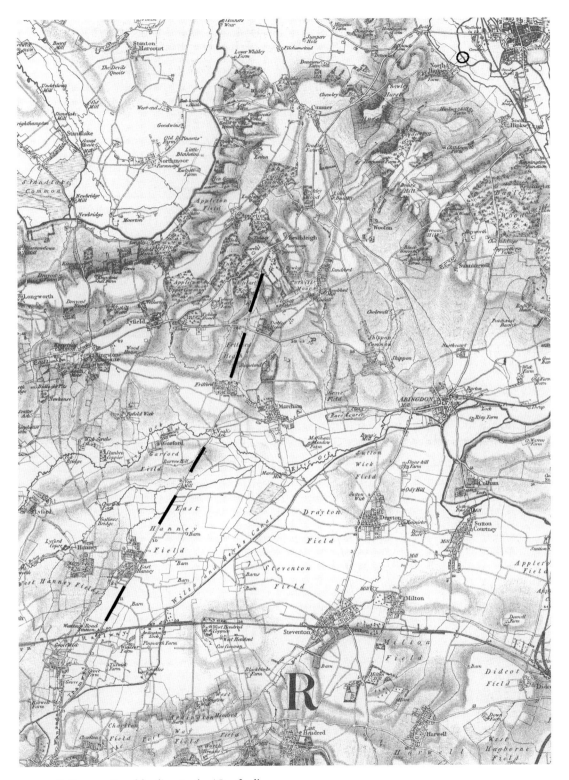

7 Roman Road leading to the 'Ox-ford'

Our presumed Roman road crosses the westernmost stream and continues as a footpath on a low causeway (*9a*) for another 300m to the next channel, the Bulstake stream, and simply stops here. Its line seemed to aim at the old Radcliffe Infirmary or St Giles' church at the northern tip of the medieval town. As we shall see (p.23), there was an important centre here in early Saxon times, though it is not clear how long this site by St Giles' church continued as a local centre. In the fourteenth century a myth, repeated in the seventeenth, called the area *Bellositum*, 'the beautiful place', and asserted that it was the site of the university long ago.

From Carfax Tower at the central crossroads, we can look above the crowds and traffic and see, above the roofs, towers and spires, a gap of low-lying ground, then greenery and low wooded hills, no more than 2km away to the west, south and east. To the south the eastern hills come down close to the Thames at Sandford-on-Thames, as do the western hills at Kennington. On a clear morning, above them far to the south, the distant line of the Berkshire Downs is sometimes visible. To the north a long low-lying tongue of gravel carries the wooded gardens of North Oxford, and then farmland rising gently to the Cotswolds. In the low-lying ground on the other three sides, two rivers, with several crossings, not easy to see from Carfax Tower, almost surround the centre of Oxford. To the west and south the Thames flows in a wide flood-plain and to the east the Cherwell flows in one, two or three channels in its narrower valley. These flood-plains of river silt with their occasional low gravel islands restrict development and contribute greatly to the city's character. They have always made defence easy and communication difficult. Going round clockwise with a map (*8*) we can note eight river-crossings, most of which, at one time or another, have been hailed as *the* ford after which Oxford was named. A: to the north-east at Holywell Mill; Hearne supposed that a Roman road from Headington crossed the Cherwell and went past the University Parks and the Roman sites that did in fact exist there. B: for the last 1,000 years the main road east from Oxford seems to have crossed the Cherwell in very much the same place as the present Magdalen Bridge. Just to the south, weapons and stirrups of Viking type were dredged up in both channels of the river in the 1880s with, it was said, the bones of men and of horses, dramatic discoveries claimed as evidence of Viking burials, or of a fierce battle there, or perhaps lost by a couple of Saxon farmers falling off their horses at the ford or bridge on their way home after a merry evening. C: some 200m south of Magdalen Bridge both streams of the Cherwell could be crossed by Milham Ford, where temporary bridges replaced the fords in the 1520s and the 1770s. D: another closed road was discovered 400m to the west in Christ Church when the foundations of Meadow Buildings were laid in 1863; the clerk of works, Mr Conradi, recorded and planned a stone-paved ford, leading north through the medieval Town Wall to Oriel Street, the medieval Shidyard Street, and south, perhaps, to wharves and boatyards beneath the grass of Christ Church mead-

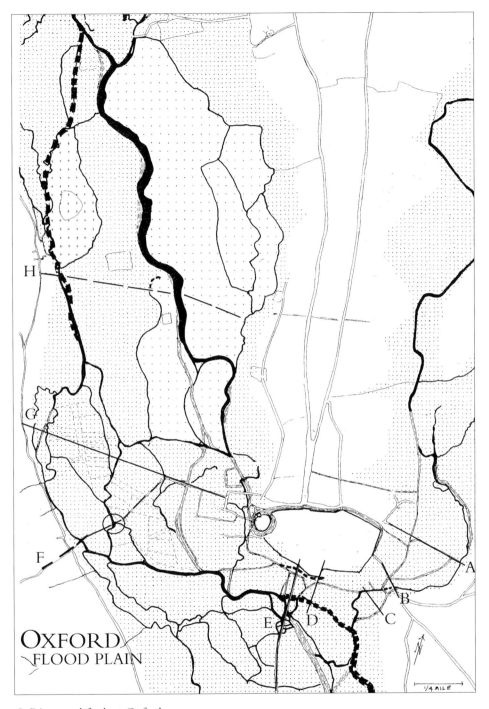

8 Rivers and fords at Oxford

9a-b Above & Opposite Aerial photographs by G.W.G. Allen, 1933, showing the 'Ox-ford' and the Roman Road; and Grandpont, a bridge and causeway of *c.*1080 leading south from the town

ow; this route may have led further south across the main stream of the Thames. E, 200m to the west Grandpont, the medieval name of the south part of St Aldate's and the north end of the Abingdon Road, is a narrow many-arched stone causeway, well-documented as the work of Robert d'Oilli in about AD 1080; now the main route from Oxford to the south, it runs ruler-straight for 600m from St Aldate's church to Western Road. The straightness alone strongly suggests that the causeway was constructed all at one time on a new line; the causeway has been widened, heightened, tunnelled into and dug up for drains and cables, but is still not lost or entirely hidden, since we can see, and even take a punt through, three low arches just south of Folly Bridge. Excavation carried out around the stone causeway in the last 30 years has revealed all kinds of features, layers of silt, casual deposits of stone, a few tim-ber posts and some basketwork barriers, which can all be explained as wharfs, mooring-posts, fish-weirs and so on of various dates, most of them after the 1080s. They are not, except to devotees of myth, evidence of a Thames cross-ing older than the city. F, the 'Ox-Ford' of medieval times, 1,500m to the west, has already been noted (pp.7-8, 16-18). G, the Botley Road, 500m north of that again, crosses the broad flood-plain of the Thames on long stone causeways of three different dates: the once narrow western section of the 1530s, widened in the 1760s and the 1930s; the middle part, from Binsey Lane to Hollybush Row, built by Oseney Abbey in around 1210; and at the east, Park End Street and New Road cut through as a coach-road in 1769. H, to the north-west the old antiquaries fantasised about a crossing from *Bellositum* by St Giles' church, leading to Binsey and the medieval village of Seacourt. Some of these crossings are not fully understood; others, like the last, have an element of fantasy.

Oxford's myths are enjoyable, ridiculous, or harmless, but some distort and betray a true understanding of history: 'Our streets ran with the red blood of hundreds of murdered Danes' is a typical over-egged Victorian elaboration of the events of AD 1002. We can try to eradicate myths but, as soon as any one of them has been conclusively disproved and shown to be fantasy, an old one will spring to new life, or a new one will form. Every city has its own myths about gold, ghosts, tunnels and often some local speciality. Oxford's special myths range from Danes to grid-plans. Myths about gold are universal. In June 1963 my colleague at the Ashmolean Museum, J.D.A. Thompson of the Coin Room, mentioned to me, an assistant keeper of antiquities, that he had been told about 'a bucket-full of gold spade-guineas' found by builders at Christ Church. I dashed down to my college on my bike, to learn from the clerk of works that workmen cleaning out 'Mercury', the goldfish pond in Tom Quad,

had picked up £5 6s 0d in low-value coins, mostly coppers, thrown in by tourists over the last few years. Myths of this sort spring up every year or two in most cities and towns; but woe betide the museum curator who fails to check up on every one. I never had the luck to track down late Saxon silver pennies by the dozen while drinking beer in seedy pubs, as happened to an acquaintance when he was a museum curator in Chester. Another myth or fantasy, that Oxford was planned on a grid in Saxon times, has sprung up like a weed at various times, always hailed as a new discovery. It was suggested in 1859 and 1914, promoted again in 1970 for much of Wessex, developed in 1971, and applied to Oxford in 1972. It is now disregarded in Winchester, where, we were assured in 1971, 'The medieval and modern street plan, although not of Roman origin... displays a regular arrangement on a grid pattern.' The 'four main components' of the supposed plan there were (i) the High Street; (ii) the back streets; (iii) the north-south streets; and (iv) the street which, in places, runs just inside the defences. Similar features in other towns 'were part of a deliberate policy of urban foundation', with the 'rectilinear street plan' showing that the town sites were shared out for 'permanent settlement' in the time of king Alfred (AD 871-899) and his son Edward the Elder (899-924). Since then it has become clear that far more of the present street-pattern of Winchester follows the Roman streets, and also that the north–south streets have a complex history and were not laid out at any one time. When the myth was born, it should have been quite obvious that there was no 'grid-pattern', no 'rectilinear street plan' at Winchester. In 1976 a new strain of the weed, the 'flint-knapping myth', claimed that 'all the streets belonged to the original layout' and that 'the initial laying of the 8.6km of surfacing... required something like 8,000 tonnes of flint cobbles' to make the small broken flints on the first roads, a fantastic and quite unrealistic calculation. In 1994 the Oxford version of the 'grid' myth was further elaborated: 'Around the year 900 a grid-plan town, with ramparts, gates and streets, was built at the north end of the 'oxen-ford', enclosing the church or churches of St. Frideswide's minster'. We have been assured, of Oxford and elsewhere, that 'The burghal towns of King Alfred's time were built by expert surveyors and engineers, who developed techniques for setting out the streets, laying down metalling and building the defences. Oxford shows clear evidence for these techniques, and was undoubtedly built in a deliberate, planned campaign...' But this is just another myth.

1

ORIGINS & GROWTH
AD 400-1200

Oxford has been occupied, perhaps continuously, since early Anglo-Saxon times. The main early settlement, perhaps known by some other name, lay at the bottom of the Woodstock Road, just past the last houses of the medieval north suburb by St Giles' church or, in a Georgian setting, around the Radcliffe Infirmary and the Royal Oak pub. By AD 450-500 a Saxon chief or princeling had a hall and burial-mounds there, and probably peasant farms nearby. In the twelfth century the land where the Infirmary stands was called the 'Croft of the Three Barrows'. These barrows were no doubt Saxon burial-mounds. Finds from the area include, in 1646, an ornamental gold disc or 'bracteate', perhaps a badge of office (*colour plate 2*); in 1770, two burials, one with a silvered or tinned iron 'plate', perhaps a shield-boss; and in 1938, a bone 'thread-picker' typical of Saxon sites, now in the Ashmolean Museum with the bracteate. We have mentioned the old myth that calls this area *Bellositum*, 'the beautiful place', the site of the university in ancient times. There were other Saxon chiefs living in the region. Cutha, or Cuthwine, gave his name to Cuddesdon, 'Cuthwine's hill', to the east of the city and to Cutteslowe, 'Cuthwine's burial-mound', to the north. He appears in the early, semi-legendary, section of the *Anglo-Saxon Chronicle*, the dynastic record of the kings of Wessex, as a war leader who, with his brother Ceawlin, captured Benson and Eynsham, both in Oxfordshire, and other towns to the east and west in the 570s and was killed in battle in 584. To understand the development of Oxford, we should glance at other towns not too far away and compare their growth in Saxon and early medieval times with Oxford's. Cambridge and Northampton each have an Iron Age hill-fort and a Roman town nearby, indicating that authority on the Cam and the upper Nene had long been located in the immediate area of the later towns. Cambridge, a small Roman town north of the Cam, may have been abandoned and later re-established as a local capital; early Saxon cemeteries have been found around the Roman town and also within and near the medieval town over the Cam to the south. Similar finds show that Northampton was a local centre by AD 500.

A second stage of Oxford's development may have been as a trading place or fairground. For a long time the sole evidence was a coin of king Offa of Mercia (757-796), reputedly found in 1841 in the foundations of the Martyrs' Memorial, at the south end of Oxford's medieval north suburb, a notably wide street very like the main street of many market towns. The penny, rather a puzzle as an isolated find, was hidden for decades in a private collection known for odd and interesting findspots and is now in the Ashmolean Museum. The find became less of a puzzle in 1999, when a few sherds of Ipswich ware, also of Middle Saxon date, were found at the Sackler Library in St John Street, 200m from the memorial. More finds of this period, perhaps similar sherds of pottery, may turn up unrecognised in museum storerooms or come to light in new excavations. By the eleventh century, if not long before, Oxford had very close links with Headington, now a suburban village within the city, then one of seven great royal estates from which the county was administered through the hundred courts, a system perhaps going back to the ninth or tenth centuries. Headington parish was large, including a lesser village and chapel at Marston and hamlets at Barton and Wick, and covered at least 1500ha, with the water meadows on the west, or Oxford, side of the Cherwell, and also the meadows south-west of the castle and Oseney Abbey, including Bulstake Mead and the 'Ox-ford'. If it included north and central Oxford, there may have been 2000ha in the parish.

A century after Offa, king Alfred of Wessex, the last of the old English kingdoms, built a fort at Oxford, or so we may reasonably deduce. Over the centuries many legends have linked Alfred the Great with Oxford (86), as the founder or re-founder of the university, or at least of University College. Alfred came to the throne in a generation of turmoil in this country and of half a century of fear and unrest in Europe. In 874 Cambridge had been seized by three Viking kings who stayed for a year, while another Viking force over-ran the kingdom of Mercia and drove the last king to exile in Rome. Viking armies seized Northumbria and East Anglia, and took control of eastern Mercia. In the west of Mercia, a great nobleman, Ethelred, kept or won back his ancestral lands along the Severn valley and sealed an alliance with Alfred by marrying his daughter, Ethelfleda. Oxford first appears in written form as OHSNAFORDA on coins minted for Alfred in the 890s by the moneyer Bernwald. In 911 the *Anglo-Saxon Chronicle*, by this time a reliable record, noted that:

> Ethelred ealdorman in Mercia died and King Edward took possession of London-burg and Oxford and all the lands which belonged to them.

London was both a Roman walled city, abandoned in early Saxon times, and also a large new trading area to the west, prosperous in middle Saxon times. The Vikings took or raided London several times, no doubt plundering the traders while using the Roman walls as a fort. In 886 Alfred captured London and handed it to ealdorman Ethelred to govern as part of a great province which included all or most of the Severn and Thames valleys, acting as regent of English-held Mercia and also as governor for the king of Wessex. The most likely year for the construction of a fort at Oxford seems to be 895, when a series of long-range Viking raids up the Thames ceased. We should imagine king Alfred, with Ethelred and another Mercian ealdorman, Ethelferth, as the local governor (and perhaps also Ethelfleda, who was then about 25), choosing the site, laying out the defences, supervising peasants brought in to dig ditches and erect a stockade. No one in this age, whether English, Viking, Frank or of any other people in Europe, looked on a fort or 'burh' as anything more than a stockade, hastily put up to create a stronghold and mustering-place for defence or attack. The best-documented English fortress of the period is Buckingham where, for 914, the *Chronicle* records that Edward the Elder, Alfred's son and successor, spent four weeks making a double fort on both sides of the river. Buckingham has no sign either of defences or of grid-planned streets.

But we can be sure that the inauguration of a fort, however makeshift, was a solemn matter, involving a religious ceremony, with the king and his retinue, his bishops and their priests, his nobles and their warriors marching in procession round the fort singing psalms while they asked Almighty God to keep it safe, halting for prayers at each gate. In this clash of cultures the Vikings may, in the 870s, have solemnised their fort at Northampton with equal ceremony, perhaps sacrificing a captured bishop or abbot who had failed to get his ransom paid in time. At Cambridge a chilling find near St Giles' church, reported in August 2003, of five decapitated skeletons 'and a sixth tied up and buried face down' under an early church, might be such a sacrifice. When Ethelred of Mercia died in 911, his widow Ethelfleda, Alfred's daughter, took over his role as the great English warlord in the Midlands and took the war into Viking-held territories. A version of the *Chronicle* tells of her setting up ten forts between 910 and 915, at Bridgnorth, Tamworth, Stafford, Warwick, Runcorn and other places. In 916 she sent her warriors into Wales to avenge the murder of one of her abbots. They brought back hostages, including the wife of the king of Brecon. In 917 Ethelfleda's warriors stormed the Viking stronghold of Derby with heavy loss and in 918 the army of Leicester submitted to her, as the Vikings of York agreed to, but ratted on the deal when she died that year, in her late forties. Meanwhile her brother, Edward the Elder, campaigned vigorously against the Vikings in the East Midlands and East Anglia, capturing some forts and putting up others. During his campaigns Northampton was the Viking fort nearest Oxford, 70km to the south-east. The *Chronicle* relates for 914 that:

> After Easter the armies of Northampton and Leicester flouted the truce and went
> on a raid, killing many people around Hook Norton [in north Oxfordshire] and
> thereabouts. As they withdrew they joined another force raiding towards Luton.
> Our men heard of this, fought them and drove them off, seizing their booty and
> of their weapons and horses.

In March 920, the *Chronicle* notes, Edward built and manned a fort at Towcester.
Four months later, in July,

> the vikings from Leicester and Northampton and further north broke the
> cease-fire and attacked and assaulted Towcester, but our warriors held out until
> reinforcements arrived and the enemy retreated.

In October, when Edward improved the defences at Towcester,

> Jarl Thurferth with his captains and all the army of Northampton as far as the
> river Welland, submitted and offered the king their allegiance.

These campaigns advanced English territory far to the north and east.

Warlike preparations were not confined to this country. In Germany the
ninth and tenth centuries are known as the *Burgwallzeit*, 'the hill-fort period';
and, among hundreds of forts built all over Europe, there are many parallels for
the 'forts' in England. We must note a special one, well known to English
churchmen, warriors, envoys and rulers of the ninth century. On 27 June 852
at Rome Pope Leo IV inaugurated his 'Leonine City', a defensive wall around
St Peter's, hastily built of brick and stone pillaged from ancient ruins to protect what remained of the imperial city from the Arab pirates who had sacked
it in 846. Some lengths of Leo's walls survive today. While they were going up,
king Ethelwulf of Wessex sent generous donations with, in 853, his youngest
son Alfred. In 855 he went in person, with Alfred, to see how his money had
been spent on this work of piety. Every stretch of badly-built wall had an
inscription naming the local estate which built it. At each gate an inscribed
poem in high-flown bad Latin repeated and exaggerated the sentiments of the
prayers chanted there in 852. The worst poem was at the *Posterula Saxonum*,
the south gate by the *Scola Saxonum* or 'saxon hostel' where English pilgrims
stayed. Part of a similar Latin inscription was found in 1902 at Malmesbury,
one of Alfred's forts, and later lost. Carved in 880, it had distinctive features of
Italian inscriptions of the period, including a square 'C' and an 'O' with a serif.
Throughout Europe Christian rulers had to defend their lands and fight back,
not always successfully, against Magyars from the east, Arabs from the south and
Vikings from the north. To the south-east the pagan Bulgars threatened the
Byzantine Empire. When the emperor Nicephoros invaded their land in 811

and burnt down their capital, except for the stone palace at its centre, he and his army were annihilated and the Bulgar ruler, Khan Krum (802-814), used the emperor's skull as a drinking cup. In Spain the small Christian kingdom of the Asturias built forts against the Arabs who had conquered most of the peninsula. In the 850s king Ordoño I, Ethelwulf's contemporary, built a line of five forts beyond the limits of his territory, just as Alfred's son and daughter did. An Asturian charter of 60 years later tells us how one of the local counts involved in this advance moved families and flocks from his own province to the new land, where he built houses for them, shared out farmland, ploughed and sowed crops and planted vines. Such movements of peasants to provide resources for new forts may have been usual in Christian, and also, no doubt, pagan lands.

We have noted and must repeat that a fort of this time was a mustering-place for local forces. It did not require markets, gravelled streets, shops, houses or churches, as some writers claim. In around 895-900 Oxford may have consisted simply of a stockade and ditch, perhaps with some internal subdivisions. The fort defence may have run somewhat south of the medieval Town Wall. When Exeter College rebuilt its chapel in 1856, one of the fellows watched the foundations and noted that:

> As part of an old City Ditch ran close to the north side, very deep foundations were required, and many cartloads of stone besides all the stone work of the old Chapel were used in these foundations.

Another possibility is that the stockade was on the line of the Town Wall. Along this line, north of St Michael Street and Ship Street and south of George Street, Broad Street and Holywell Street, a rampart of turf and gravel has been observed and excavated, continuing on the east and south of the medieval town. The date of this defence, sometimes thought to be the 'original' defence of the 'burh', is not clear. It survived for centuries in ghostly form as a strip of land behind the Wall, leased out in sections by the town council. In 1912 H.E. Salter sensibly pointed out that it must represent 'a mound of earth inside the wall', but it took 50 years for this to be confirmed. In 1957 a group of students, of whom I was one, tried to find and date the Town Wall by digging a trench in a cellar 30m west of Northgate. Expecting to find a stone wall, we were puzzled to find a thick deposit of red-brown loam with a few lumps of coral ragstone and thick-headedly failed to realise that it was Salter's 'mound of earth', which we should have recognised as a rampart.

In 1962 I recorded a similar thick deposit of red-brown loam in the foundation-trench of a new building at Exeter College (*10*). As I drew the section, I realised that it was a rampart of turf and gravel, and wondered how we had failed to make sense of it five years before. In 1963 I noted a similar deposit in the foundations of the warden's lodgings at Merton College. The rampart has

10 Saxon rampart at Exeter College; P.R.S. Moorey, later keeper of antiquities, Ashmolean Museum, examining the old surface, on the site of Margary Quad, 1962

since been observed at Pembroke College in 1973, St Michael's church in 1975, St Michael Street in 1985, New College in 1993, and the castle in 2003-4. This defence line, perhaps of the tenth century, was clearly followed by the Town Wall except on the south through Merton and Christ Church, where it has not yet come to light. Yet another possible defence line, perhaps of the eleventh century, follows the parish boundary between St Mary Magdalen and St Giles, later the boundary of Northgate hundred, 300m to the north of the medieval Town Wall. A large ditch is documented in thirteenth-century deeds at Durham, recording the Cathedral monks' purchase of arable fields as a site for their college, now Trinity, and in sixteenth-century deeds at St John's about land bought to extend the garden. This ditch was observed when a water tank was dug in St John's North Quad in 1943 and, across the street to the west, the line is shown by a large stone drain, which may represent a ditch, discovered in extending Blackfriars in 1951. No stockade or rampart has yet been found on this line. The interior of the fort may have been divided up with ditches, hedges or fences into blocks assigned to local landowners. Three sections of ditch have been observed at various times; at Brasenose College in 1959 a north–south ditch, 12.5m long and dug 0.9-1.5m into natural gravel was succeeded by a rubble wall between 22 and 23 High Street. Under Church Street in 1969-70 a north–south ditch, 9m long and dug 1.25m into natural gravel, may have been more than 47m long. An east–west ditch found north of Castle Street in 1970-2 was 'at least 0.7m deep' at two points 43m apart. Within the subdivisions local lords may have put up huts for retainers, perhaps also for their peasants in time of trouble, later adding barns, store-houses, stables and such things as workshops and forges for swordsmiths.

Oxford, an abandoned military base, became a town between 900 and 1200. I am sure, although it is controversial to say so, that the process was a gradual one, without any master plan or by order of any single authority; that landowners laid out streets as and where they chose, and that properties were cut through by lanes and subdivided into house plots and small shop plots over a very long period. In the last 50 years a mass of archaeological evidence has come to light, resulting in several large bodies of finds and records dispersed around local museum stores. But there is no general agreement, and probably never will be, on matters as diverse and important as the location of the fort defences, the origin of the streets, the dating of pottery and so on. Since the 1890s a vast mass of documentary evidence, mainly title-deeds, has filled thousands of pages of volumes of the Oxford Historical Society, often completely in Latin. It is not easy to extract useful information from the deeds, still less combine it sensibly with the archaeological conclusions or notions.

In 1958 E.M. Jope, Belfast-based archaeologist and former Oxford bio-chemist, and W.A. Pantin, church historian and college tutor, published a detailed report on the archaeology and buildings of a large site in Cornmarket, the old-fashioned Clarendon Hotel rebuilt in 1954-6 as a large Woolworths, now a shopping mall. Lately described as 'the single most important excavation of late Saxon remains in Oxford', it produced 11 cellar-pits of about 950-1200,

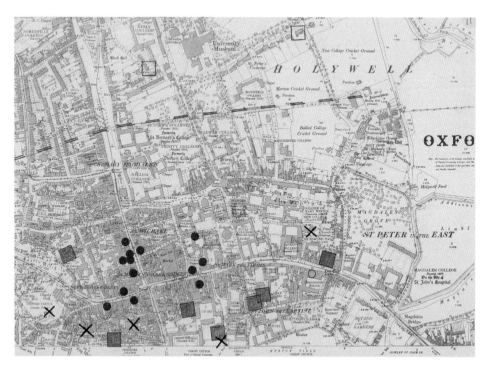

11 Oxford, late Saxon cellar-pits found in 1870 (circle) and 1954-2004 (black circles), post-holes of surface-built huts (Xs), line of large, possibly defensive, ditch (dashes), and major building-sites not investigated 1965-85 (grey squares)

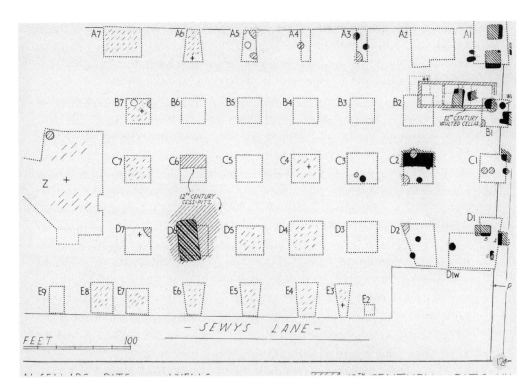

12a-b Cellar-pits at the Clarendon Hotel, 1954-5: *a) Above* Plan of 1959; *b) Below* Revised plan

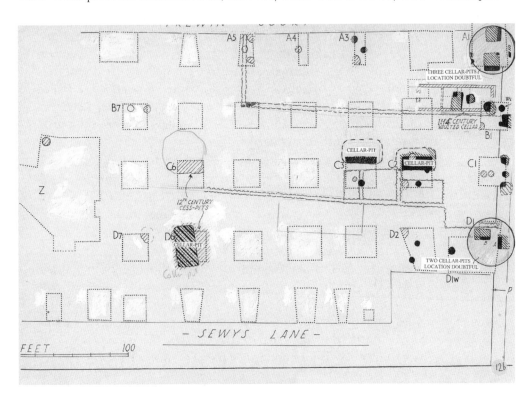

perhaps the largest group of these typical and characteristic features to have been found in Britain. Fifty years ago, as a 19-year-old classics student who had been on a few digs, I drew most of the published site-records, sketching layers and features. Scrabbling about for pottery, I recovered most of the stratified finds and vividly remember the chaotic circumstances. The report is full of discrepancies and omissions and urgently needs to be reassessed. In medieval times Oseney Abbey owned much of the site with many shops and houses close by; Pantin ignored much vital information about the site and the street which was available among the thousand Oseney charters, Oxford's richest group of medieval deeds, published by H.E. Salter less than 30 years before. Jope's site plan differs so much from the contractors' foundation plan that the exact location of six of the 11 cellar-pits must be considered doubtful (*12a-b*). I sometimes wonder why Jope, with exact copies of my field notes, altered my observations in his published plans and sections, as with the street-metalling of Cornmarket, where I observed three very thick gravel levels, the uppermost and latest of which extended slightly further west; but his published version shows five or six layers of gravelling encroaching progressively on the occupation layers of the site. Cellar-pits, easy enough to recognise, have turned up at Canterbury, Chester, London, Northampton and York. In Oxford about 30 have been recorded, most of them in 1955-70, in a hectic time of discovery in the main shopping streets (*11*). The sites of these discoveries can be identified, as readily as the cellar-pits themselves, as faceless modern shops built for chains like Littlewoods or Marks & Spencer, since sold on. In Oxford cellar-pits do not seem to occur on the side streets, but lie in two, three or even four ranks along the main streets. They come in four sizes; large, medium, small and very small sunken huts, together with a fair number of partly-exposed 'probables', 'possibles' and 'doubtfuls'. The large cellar-pits perhaps took up, below ground, the whole area of a building that stood above ground, providing a large cool storage area. The medium and small cellar-pits may have lain below part of a building, or beneath a very small structure, used no doubt as a larder.

One of the smallest, a shallow sunken hut, D18 at 55-8 Cornmarket (then Littlewoods) on the west side of the street, of a type familiar on settlements of early and mid-Saxon times, was only 2.8m long and perhaps 1.8m wide (*13b*); perhaps of the tenth century or earlier, it was dug 25-28cm into the natural red-brown loam, but not into the natural gravel below, and had a gravel floor, on which rested timber fragments, perhaps from wattle or matting and a thin layer of grey loamy clay. At the east end of the hut a posthole held the impression of its post, and the south side was clearly defined by a wood-stain and two stake-holes, south of which an area of natural red-brown loamy topsoil was cut by a gully or beam-slot parallel to the wood-stain, five postholes and 23 stake-holes, some of which probably belonged to the superstructure of the hut. The red-brown loamy fill of the hut contained no pottery, no other finds and no indication of date.

13a-d In the cellars of 55-8 Cornmarket:

a) *Above* Student volunteers, including a future inspector of ancient monuments

b) *Below* A section of sunken hut D18

c) *Opposite above* Large cellar-pit B1, with earlier pits truncated when it was dug, in around the eleventh century

d) *Opposite below* Pit A1, filled with fire-debris during clearance in the eleventh or twelfth century. *Photos, 1962*

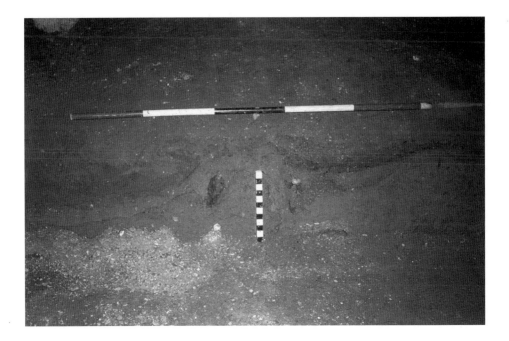

14a-b Late Saxon features at 23-5 Queen Street; *a*) *Above* Cellar-pit A1 and beam-slot A2; both features, dug into yellow natural gravel, projected beyond the street front at base of view; *b*) *Below* Sunken hut or cellar-pit A7 and postholes. The beam-slot and postholes seem to represent buildings standing over the cellar-pits. *Photos, 1960*

The area was part of a very large property which king Canute gave to Abingdon Abbey in 1032, when it included St Martin's church and was the home of one Ethelwine. In the 1150s Abingdon leased it, no doubt reduced to a large merchant's house, to Ralf the Breton, from whom it passed to the wealthy Henry son of Simeon, whose younger son Stephen married the heiress to the barony of Cogges. His elder son, a second Henry Simeon, sold the property to Adam Feteplace, mayor 14 times in 1244-67, and his son, Walter Feteplace, had inherited it by 1279. The modern site, assembled in the nineteenth century by Grimbly Hughes, grocers, was rebuilt in 1962 for Littlewoods, whose former store is now a McDonald's restaurant and other shops.

In the north side of the same site a large cellar-pit B1, perhaps of the eleventh century, was 9m long by 4.5m wide (*13c*). The most completely excavated of Oxford's large cellar-pits, it was dug only 1m into the natural gravel towards the street front and somewhat more, 1.45m, at the back. Impressions of a timber lining survived in places. It had been dug through seven earlier pits and, like the nearby pit A1, was filled with burnt debris, including much pottery, a pottery lamp, a knife, a buckle, pieces of lead and a silver penny of Aethelred II (979-985). None of this material could be relied on to show when the cellar was dug, how long it was used, nor when it fell out of use. The house above and all the surrounding buildings had evidently burnt down. The area was then levelled and the remains and floor-levels of the houses were

15 A vital observation: a twelfth-century beam-slot on the present street frontage of 13-21 Cornmarket. *Photo, 1960*

simply shovelled into the cellar. This part of the site was half of a large merchant property owned in the mid-twelfth century by Snelling, his son Sewi, and then his grandson or great-grandson John Sewi (bailiff in 1239). Sewi also had sons Roger {16} and Nicholas {43}*. Another large cellar-pit, recorded at the Clarendon Hotel in 1955, lay 48m back from the street front, was aligned north–south and dug deep into natural gravel. It was later truncated by a large rubbish pit or cesspit, about 9.2m across, filled with stinking black silt full of old shoes, leather-clippings and pottery of about the late twelfth century. At that time this part of the site belonged to Lambert son of Thovi, *alias* Lambert the cordwainer, a prominent citizen who held the highest civic office as one of the two bailiffs in the 1170s, before Oxford had a mayor. He was one of the town's two aldermen in 1181 and still in 1190, when he may have died in office. To judge from the leather fragments that I salvaged from the site in my student days and wrote up in my early months at the Ashmolean Museum, his shoe business included much repair work. The house passed to a great merchant, Thomas Feteplace, his son Walter, and his grandson, another Thomas Feteplace who was living there in 1279 at the time of Hundred Rolls survey.

A third large cellar-pit at the Clarendon Hotel came to light in 1955, too late to save the hotel from destruction. Of great architectural interest, it was 13m long by 4.5m wide, and dug 60cm into the natural gravel from a much higher level. It did not require excavation as it had served as the hotel wine vault for many years and was lined, not with timber, but with mortared rubble walls 60cm thick (*16*), which largely survive below ground. About two-thirds of the way back, or 8.4m from the outer face of the front wall, it was crossed by an arch on imposts with a simple moulding, probably of about 1070-1100. Pantin and Jope dated it to 1150-70 but concluded that much of the south wall was rebuilt and a barrel-vault inserted in the thirteenth or fourteenth century, leaving the earlier arch in place, a judgement which might be reconsidered. The cellar, dug through three earlier pits or wells, lay entirely behind the modern street front. In 1184-98 Oseney leased the area of the cellar and a much wider property behind, described as 'all the land which Richard the Breton held from us', to Hugh son of William Husar {53}, except for two shops. The buildings on the property were listed as:

> Two solars, oak framed and tiled, two cellars, one *ad votam* [perhaps a misreading], the other planked, and a hall within, with a thatched roof. If anything in the said cellar or solar over it deteriorates, we will repair whatever needs mending beneath the planking. But the tenant is to repair whatever is needed above the planking, or the planking itself.

*These brackets refer to the Charter of 1191; see pp.38 and 65

16 Stone vaulted cellar at the Clarendon Hotel, 52-53 Cornmarket, with arch of *c*.1080 and vault of *c*.1300, from the east. *Photo by Alun Jones, 1955*

Immediately to the south was another large property, noted on a deed of 1170-84 as having 'two cellars'; the lessee, Owen the vintner {28}, bailiff of Oxford in about 1195, no doubt kept an inn here. Three large stone-lined cellars with no datable features lay along the south side of this property, from 9.15m to 29.6m back from the modern frontage; they may still partly survive today. In the 1950s Pantin, as buildings expert, assumed that they were 'modern' and did not examine them because they were below ground, and Jope, the archaeologist, ignored them too, because they were full of air, not layers of gravel and earth. They may well have been twelfth- or thirteenth-century, remaining in use until the twentieth. Just to the west of the Clarendon Centre, under Frewin Hall, a large vaulted cellar of about 1080-1120 survives, now three bays long, with a barrel-vault over the western bay and rough groined vaults over the other two. Unevenly placed 3.35m from the present west wall a massive column, of around 1120 to judge from its capital, was evidently inserted, to support a hearth or partition on the upper floor. The cellar measures 14.5m by 5m; but may have been 25m long when it was built. It seems to have been the home of the local magnate and county sheriff Henry of Oxford, who owned other property in Oxford and Wallingford and rural estates nearby. The house above was rebuilt in around 1600 and much altered in the 1880s.

The scale of building to be anticipated in mid- and late Saxon deposits on town sites is most uncertain. A far grander stone hall, excavated at Northampton in 1980-2, was 37.6m long by 11.4m wide and stood on the site of an earlier timber hall 29.7m long by 8.6m wide. Both were presumably built for a great noble or king. The excavator's date of around 850, ascribed to the stone hall on the basis of Carbon-14 samples, may be too early. The early inhabitants of Oxford seem to have lived and carried on trade and manufacture at first in scattered huts and houses. By the 1190s the main streets were built up with continuous frontages of houses and shops of varied forms, built with all sorts of materials and techniques. The main building materials were wood and earth, as solid cob walling or daubed onto basketwork or wattle panels, although an early house with rubble walls has also been found. Evidence for the above-ground parts of houses has been observed or excavated, often fragmentary and hard to make sense of and reconstruct. Timber posts were sometimes set into postholes dug into the ground, and sometimes into horizontal timbers or sill-beams. In 1960 a beam-slot, a row of postholes and a mass of scattered postholes were found in the surface of the natural gravel at 23-5 Queen Street near a sunken hut and a cellar-pit (*14*).

In 1191 62 leading townsmen, many of them with houses in the town centre, put their names to a charter granting Medley to Oseney Abbey, sealing it confidently with their corporate seal, perhaps the earliest in the country. In this chapter a bracketed number, such as { *15* }, shows their place among the names on the charter. As well as these prosperous citizens, perhaps mostly merchants, the descendants or successors of local landowners who were assigned blocks of land when the fort was founded in the 890s (pp.27-8), may still have received rents and dues from them. In 1005 ealdorman Aethelmaer gave Eynsham Abbey, as part of the foundation endowments

> his court (*curiam*) in Oxford in which was situated the church of St Ebbe with certain other rents pertaining to the court

and two mills next to Oxford and meadows. In 1034 king Canute gave Abingdon Abbey the village of Lyford, then in Berkshire,

> and a certain little-minster consecrated in honour of St Martin, bishop, with the adjacent small-estate (*cum adjacenti praediolo*) in the town which is called by the famous name Oxnaford.

In 1086, Domesday Book named 30 local landowners with Oxford properties attached to their estates. The king himself had a house in Oxford attached to the great royal manor of Shipton-under-Wychwood in west Oxfordshire and another belonging to Bloxham to the north-west; he had a house attached to Princes Risborough and two more to Twyford, both in Buckinghamshire. In Domesday Book these houses

> are called wall-houses because if there is need and the king commands it, they will repair the wall.

House-owners included the archbishop of Canterbury, who owned Newington south-east of Oxford and no other Oxfordshire property, and the abbot of Bury St Edmunds with a house attached to Taynton on the Gloucestershire border. In the twelfth century a large property at 23-26 Queen Street was attached to Deddington in north Oxfordshire, while another at 13-21 Cornmarket (p.41, *15*), had links with Pyrton, south-east of Oxford. These other house properties may have retained links with rural estates from the 890s until the twelfth century, if most large country estates had to send workers and peasants to maintain the defences, as well as warriors to assemble there before riding out against the Vikings, or any other enemy. In 1227, when the young Henry III, who had just declared himself to be of age, tried to order 34 Oxford house-owners to repair the defences, houses rather than estates had the obligation to maintain the defences. Many of their houses were in the north-east of the walled town.

In 1198 Oseney Abbey sold or leased land on the east side of Cornmarket;

> our land in St Mildred's parish between the land of Kenelm the priest and the land of Ralf of Brackley

to Ralf Coleman {24}, with

> two oak-framed houses with stone-slate roofs; one towards the open space (*platea*) with a cellar and a solar, and a horse-mill without horses or millstones in the cellar; and the other towards the yard (*curia*) with two malt-kilns (*turaillis*) and as well as these buildings which we have built. Ralf was to build other buildings at his own expense… and he has given us one besant as a pledge.

Soon afterwards Ralf Coleman, who owned another property on the north, sold this one to William the miller and his partner, Henry the miller. To the north, outside Northgate, in the 1190s Oseney gave Robert son of Sunegot the lease of a property called the 'land of Horsporte'. Now 5-8 Magdalen Street, it was a large plot containing four houses,

> A great house of stone with a cellar and solar of stone and a tiled privy and also a chamber of stone. A house of stone and earth with two stables, one of stone and one of earth. And in another part of the courtyard a chamber of stone and a house of stone and earth. And behind them in the courtyard a privy and a great house of earth. The houses are all thatched.

Much of the town had been destroyed in a great fire in 1190, so that the mention of thatch suggests that these houses had escaped the fire. The first house with its various parts was evidently built of rubble, like the cellar at 52-3 Cornmarket (*16*). The second house, 'of stone and earth' may have had rubble footings and cob walls, while one of its stables was all of rubble, the other all of cob. The third

17a-b Left & opposite Castle, a chapel often thought to be St George's church, view of crypt and plan. *Daniel Harris, 1796*

house seems to have been quite like the second, with an attached chamber all of rubble, while the fourth house, by the privy, was built of cob without footings, if we can trust this description. In the early twentieth century the whole area was rebuilt with deep basements; no finds were reported then and it is unlikely that any archaeological deposits remain.

Oxford antiquaries have always observed streets and their surfaces of gravel and limestone whenever they were dug up for pipes and drains, in the 1660s, the 1730s and notably in the 1890s. Cornmarket, then the A34 carrying all the heavy traffic from the industrial Midlands to the south coast ports, was closed for several months in 1953-4 to lay new drains. H.J. Case, prehistorian at the Ashmolean, looked down the trenches, saw bright yellow gravel extending from a depth of 60-90cm below the existing rubber-brick surface to a depth of 2-3m and assumed that this was the undisturbed natural gravel, although finds from the spoil heaps included an antler-pick, perhaps of neolithic date, two Saxon knives (*28b*) and a glazed tripod-pitcher handle of about the late twelfth century. Observations in Cornmarket and Queen Street later showed

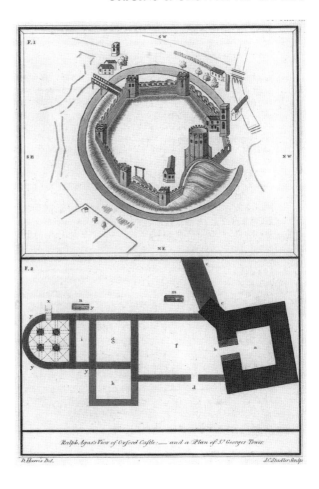

Ralph Agas's View of Oxford Castle:— and a Plan of St Georges Tower.

D. Harris Del.

J.C. Stadler Sculp.

that those streets were raised by dumping gravel, presumably from digging cellar-pits or a broad defensive ditch in a short time, or in several abrupt phases in the eleventh or twelfth centuries, when these streets were raised by as much as 1.7m. Some minor streets, by contrast, were laid out, surfaced and raised by no more than 10-30cm in about the twelfth century (*colour plate 5*). Just when the present streets were laid out and their frontages established requires careful consideration. At the Clarendon Hotel in 1955 Jope observed that several cellar-pits or wells lay partly or wholly in front of the modern street frontage and his conclusion, published in 1958, was that the street had been much narrower in Saxon times and was later widened. He assumed that cellar pits also lay beneath the roadway on the opposite side of the street. It seemed quite logical but turned out to be quite wrong. In 1959 I excavated a trench, well back from the frontage on the other side of the street, at 13-21 Cornmarket, a new Marks & Spencers store, later a Co-op, now subdivided into smaller shops. In 1960-1, while watching the foundations and basement being dug out, I found that there were no early pits or other features in a broad zone extending some 6m back from

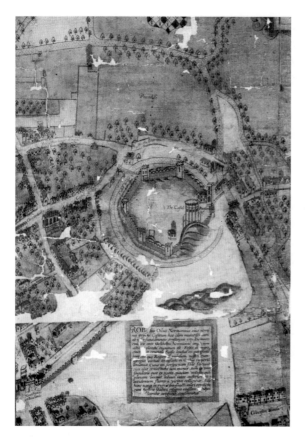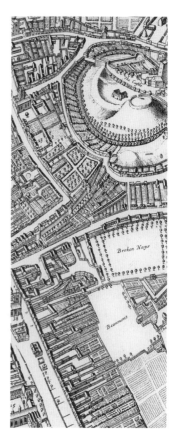

18a-b Site of the castle and palace, a single complex linked by gardens, orchards and stables. *Agas, 1578; Loggan, 1675*

the modern frontage, and concluded that the street, wider in Saxon times, had been narrowed, and perhaps re-aligned, in the twelfth century, but that at any rate the street frontages have changed very little since 1200 (*15*). The real state of affairs was more complex, as the Oseney deeds seem to show that in the late twelfth century there were rows of shops on both sides of the street with yards or vacant land between the backs of the shops and the fronts of the houses behind. The minor streets cannot be part of any 'master-plan' drawn up by a late Saxon royal adviser, as some have claimed (p.22). Most of these streets were laid out in the twelfth century across earlier house-sites. In 1960 Fabian Radcliffe (*6*) examined the lost Kybald Street and exposed three road-metallings of the twelfth-fifteenth centuries with early frontages on both sides in the form of beam-slots. Beneath the earliest road-surface he found three earlier pits. In 1963 and 1965 my digs at St Frideswide's Lane revealed much the same state of affairs (*colour plate 5*). South-west of the central crossroads at Carfax, we should scrutinise the map to investigate the supposed 'grid pattern of smaller side streets'. The block nearest Carfax, 144m long, is 150m wide at the east end and 90m at the west end, not rectangular. The side street bounding it on the south (now Pembroke Street) leaves the main road (now St

Aldate's) not at a right angle, but at about 69°. The next block on the west, 96m long, is something less than 90m wide at the east and 64m at the west; while that to the south, 102m long, is 21.5m wide at the east end and 31.5m at the west. If these blocks form a grid I am a Dutchman. All the 'smaller side streets' are distinctly curved; when surveyed on a scale of 1:500 in the 1870s, they varied in width from over 6m to less than 4m. We must conclude that the streets of central Oxford were never laid out on a grid plan, and have no real 'rectangular' or 'rectilinear' character. It was clear from findings on two main streets before 1970 that both had been re-aligned at some date. Nine minor streets have produced earlier pits, burials, levels or deposits beneath the earliest road-surfaces. By the thirteenth century there were hundreds of long narrow properties along the main streets, many with small shops on the street, while there were hundreds of shorter and wider house-plots on the back streets. This pattern must have been the result of constant minor change over a long period, as in other English towns and cities. Some changes must have taken place when an area of the town was cleared by fire or when a property owner, a monastery or a great lord, decided to redevelop his own land. During the thirteenth century, as we learn from thousands of charters, merchants, lords and monasteries constantly bought and sold the many small shops in front of their large houses in the main street, as they bought, leased and sold the houses themselves.

Oxford Castle, centre of royal authority in medieval times and of county business in modern times, lies 300m west of Carfax. The inner ward took up the west end of the walled town and has long been thought of as a small 'motte-and-bailey' castle surrounding a hall and the church of St George (p.49, *17*). The castle must have had extensive gardens, stables, barns and other service yards, as well as barbicans and outworks. We should consider the nearby royal palace, the 'new hall' or 'king's hall', as part of the castle. First recorded in 1133 and regularly documented between 1195 and 1270, it was given to the Carmelite Friars in 1318 by Edward II. Since the seventeenth century historians and antiquaries have tended to think of castle and palace as separate buildings. We must discard this view and look on the two as a single large complex, such as we can see at Guildford. In 1934 Salter's *Map of Medieval Oxford* followed Clark's map of 1889, in showing the castle as approximately oval, 180m by 110m within the walls, with a ditch about 30m wide, and the 'Carmelites' as an irregular precinct about 150m across, with a gap of 180m between the two. He filled the gap with 'Yresmanestrete' on the exact line of the present George Street and some 'Waste land' with the name 'Brokenheys'; a name first found in 1396 which implies that this part of Oxford was then semi-derelict with 'broken hedges'. This area may have been the castle gardens and orchards. George Street, pegged out in 1641 as a speculative development by a group of ambitious city fathers, cannot be the medieval 'Irishman's Street'. The dozen medieval house-plots that Salter located there must be put somewhere else. The whole royal property, castle and palace combined, may have been 550-700m long, stretching from Paradise Street in the south to St John Street in the north, and anything up to 230m wide. The southern part, the castle proper, was military with the residential ranges and gardens to the north. The castle's main surviving features, St George's Tower and the 'motte' or castle mound, a grass-covered mound 19.5m high are easy to see, and may soon be accessible to visitors. Castle mounds or 'mottes', large and small, can be found all over Europe. In England they were long believed to be the 'burhs' with which Anglo-Saxon kings defended their towns, a notion destroyed when Mrs E.S. Armitage published *Early Norman Castles of the British Isles* (1912), showing clearly that this notion was unsound. Her new theory, at once adopted by all scholars, may have been too rigid, attributing all castle mounds in England to the Norman conquerors after 1066. We were all taught at school that that early Norman castles were of 'motte-and-bailey' form and thus, by implication, relatively small. This assumption, seldom questioned over the last century, may not be valid. Castle mounds have attracted a great deal of attention and excavation, with surprising results. We cannot be sure that all Norman castles were of 'motte-and-bailey' form from the start, nor that all castles of that form are original works of Norman date. Loggan's bird's-eye view of Oxford in 1675 shows the castle as a grassy mound with a bailey or inner enclosure on the south-east (*18*). Round the top of the mound he shows a low wall and round half the inner enclosure, from the mound to an entrance from the town, a curving grass-covered bank. Some at least of this bank was an artillery-defence of 1650-1, the result of panicky defensive thinking by Colonel Draper, parliament's governor of Oxford. A century before Loggan, Agas's bird's-eye view of the city in 1578/88 shows the castle, its mound topped by a tall shell-keep, obviously of stone, and an inner enclosure surrounded, not by a grass bank or rampart, but by a high stone wall with six tall towers or bastions. One of these towers, St George's, still stands; another, the southernmost, is just where Loggan shows a low round tower; the next in the circuit, the gate from the town, is just where Loggan shows a bridge across the castle ditch and an entrance into the enclosure. Between the dates of the two views, 1578 and 1675, the stone keep and practically all the castle wall with five stone towers, thousand of tonnes of stone, were robbed out. Excavations at the castle, in advance of hotel-development, are starting to improve our scanty knowledge. Half the area of the inner enclosure, a gaol from the 1790s to the 1990s, was not easy to get at for research. Since 1769 a long strip next to the gaol has been covered by New Road, and is even more inaccessible. In 1790 the Oxford Canal Company bought a section next to this, establishing its main coal wharf there, covered with heaps of coal when I was a child in the 1940s. In 1949-60 there was intermittent salvage-archaeology, in which I played a part, when the coal was replaced by the stolid neo-Tudor stonework of Nuffield College. From 1309 to 1538 the 'king's house' further north was a Carmelite monastery, robbed and later covered by Beaumont Street, an elegant development of the 1820s, which has helped to obscure how castle and palace fitted together.

2
CHURCHES & MONASTERIES

Between 1066 and 1546 the Catholic Church used almost 60 religious buildings, crammed into the walled town and its suburbs, many with their own burial grounds. The Church of England now has 11 medieval places of worship in central Oxford. The Priory of St Frideswide, sole survivor of 10 monastic churches, is now the Cathedral of Oxford diocese and the chapel of my old college, Christ Church, which maintains and pays for it, in a unique arrangement. Six historic colleges use their medieval chapels, left from 18 old college chapels, for Anglican services, concerts and other functions. And four parish churches remain from 24 in medieval times; these and four other parish churches partly or wholly rebuilt in the nineteenth century make a great impact on the city centre, while the college chapels and the Cathedral are almost hidden behind gates and high walls. In medieval times there were also two hospital chapels, two gate-chapels and a wayside chapel. Precise totals for any category or century cannot be given, as some churches and chapels had several functions, one after the other or at the same time. Within the modern city boundary the villages of Binsey, Littlemore, and Wolvercote had churches or chapels serving outlying parts of town parishes, and there were parish churches at Cowley, Headington, Iffley and Marston. A longish walk or short ride away were three nunneries – Godstow Abbey, Littlemore Priory and Studley Priory; and the Knights Templar at Cowley and later at Sandford on Thames were part of the town's religious and social life. During the twelfth and thirteenth centuries Oxford's Jewish community had a synagogue south of Carfax in the centre of the town (2) and two successive burial-places outside Eastgate.

The monastic churches, quite well-documented from their foundation in the twelfth or thirteenth centuries, were mostly large, with organised bodies of monks, canons or friars living in cloistered courtyards by the churches. Most of the parish churches were older than the monasteries and smaller, serving families living in houses nearby; priests with parishes of 30 families cannot have found life easy depending on their offerings; others with 100 and more households, or outside funding, had a more secure income. In the twelfth to fourteenth centuries they all passed into the hands of bishops, monasteries or colleges. In the

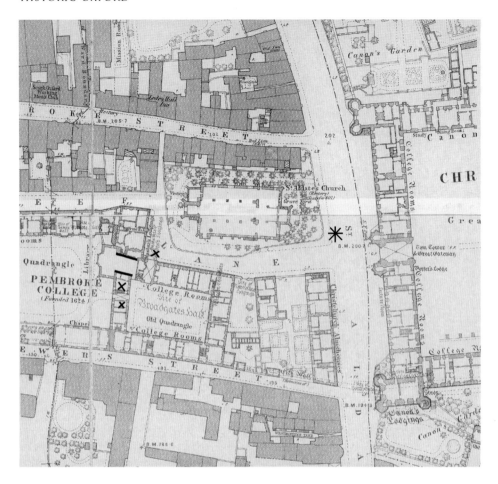

next chapter we will glance at the ancient city church, St Martin's at Carfax (pp.66-7, *26a-d, 27a-b, colour plate 13a-b*), and in the one after at the university church of St Mary the Virgin (pp.93-7, *44a-c, 45a-c, colour plate 8a-b*). We know very little about the origin of any of the parish churches, although even before 1066 no church ever just happened. Someone with a conscience, good or bad, must have decided to set it up and others must have given money, employed a carpenter if it was to be a wooden church, or found a mason if it was to be of stone. The first church at St Mary's, which may have been founded by a local thegn in the tenth or eleventh centuries, seems to have lain west of the present church (*20*). The second church, of around 1180-90, was on the present site, but differed in shape and plan from the present, largely fifteenth-century church. In 1086 Domesday Book says, under Oxford:

> A church and three properties belong to the lands which Earl Aubrey held. Two of the properties go with St Mary's church, and pay 28 pence, and the third belongs to Burford, and pays five shillings.

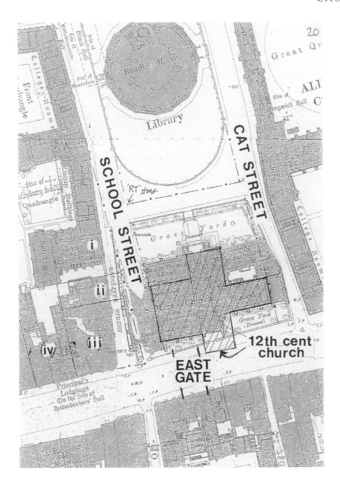

19 *Opposite* A lost church at Pembroke College? – the old hall of Broadgates Hall (p.84, walls darkened) nearby burials (marked X) and an Arabic gold coin (p.51, marked with an asterisk). The synagogue (p.11, 45, 2) stood on the site of the northern octagonal towers of Christ Church. St Michael at the Southgate stood across the main road at the end of Brewer Street, which follows the line of the Town Wall.

20 *Left* St Mary the Virgin, the 'first church' at plots i–iv, with the 'second' church of *c*.1180-90, and a possible Eastgate and former lines of Cat Street and School Street; 'RT' (p.128) marks the south-west corner of Radcliffe Trust land

Aubrey, briefly William the Conqueror's Earl of Northumbria, had been tenant-in-chief of Iffley, formerly held by Azur, and of Little Minster. He was also under-tenant of Burford on the immense holdings of the Conqueror's brother Odo, bishop of Bayeux, until he gave up his earldom and English lands to return to Europe. Azur had also held estates at Lillingstone Lovell and Chastleton, but the name was not uncommon and they may not all have belonged to the same man. Until the nineteenth century the parish of St Mary the Virgin included, not Iffley proper, but the adjoining township of Littlemore, a link that persisted for some purposes until at least the 1950s. From this and from the puzzling and difficult Domesday entries, we might deduce that the site of St Mary's and adjoining houses had formed a block of land assigned or attached to Iffley, possibly since the 890s and that a Saxon lord of Iffley founded the church for his men living nearby. Other parish churches may have a similar origin. In '1074', not a very reliable date, the leading local baron, Robert d'Oilli, endowed St George's in the Castle with St Mary Magdalen's. A layman, Edwin son of Godgose, built St Giles' in the 1120s,

obtained parochial rights, and gave it to Godstow Abbey in 1139. The churches themselves often owned some houses in the parish or nearby, sometimes
built on part of the churchyard. Some parishes, like All Saints', St Edward's,
St Michael's and St Mildred's, contained no more than 30–50 houses on 1–3ha.
Others included tracts of farmland and meadow, outside the town wall or
detached and some distance away. The two largest parishes were St Peter in the
East, owner in 1086 of two 'hides' (that is a fair-sized agricultural estate of
some 94ha) in Holywell, a hamlet just outside the town to the north-east with
its chapel of St Cross, as well as the village of Wolvercote to the north with
farmland of 298ha or so; and St Giles' with 390ha, covering the northern half
of the old north suburb with the open fields of Walton or north Oxford
(pp.86-88, *43a-b*) and meadowland. Next came St Thomas's parish, with
260ha including the medieval west suburb and meadows to the west, and St
Frideswide's parish which included both Binsey, of 154ha, still within the
medieval town limits, and Cutteslowe, of 112ha, in Wootton hundred. St
Frideswide's Priory also owned the village churches of Headington, Marston
and Elsfield north-east of the town and claimed, as quasi-parochial rights, par-
tial tithes from six villages further east and south-east; perhaps they had all been
within an ancient minster-parish.

Documents, chance finds and archaeology tell us a good deal, but there are
vast gaps in our knowledge of the parish churches. It would not be at all surprising if an unknown church, short-lived and unrecorded or only partly documented, came to light. There are three or four possible examples. In 1882 a
broken tomb-slab of the eleventh century was found at the Examination
Schools. In 1937 or '38 another fragment was found when 117-8 St Aldate's
was rebuilt. South-west of St Aldate's church, burials were found at Pembroke
College in the eighteenth century and in the 1950s on either side of the old
college dining hall, formerly the hall of Broadgates Hall (and later, from the
1840s to the 1970s, the college library). The side walls of the hall lie on a quite
different alignment and in striking unconformity to the nearby college buildings and streets, and also to St Aldate's church (*19*), making it a candidate for
a lost Saxon church. Another church which vanished, without acquiring a
parish, was built in the late 1140s by an eminent church lawyer, Walter the
archdeacon of Oxford, provost of St George's church in 1110-50 and friend of
Geoffrey of Monmouth, on his prebendal estate of Walton, north-west of the
town. Despite the bishop's prohibition, he gave it to St Frideswide's, probably
to annoy the monks of Oseney. This church, lost or aborted, may be found
when the old Radcliffe Infirmary site is redeveloped. Three parish churches,
well enough documented, have never actually been located. The first St John's
church may lie north of its successor, Merton College chapel, rather than
south, as college historians claim. The second St Budoc's church, outside
Westgate, may lie under or near the Jolly Farmers pub. I once thought that I
had found the foundations of St Michael's at Southgate which, if not dug away

by Wolsey's labourers in 1525, must lie buried in St Aldate's opposite the end of Brewer Street. Wolsey's men, working on Cardinal College, may also have destroyed all remains of the synagogue some way to the north. To these lost, failed, unlocated or half-located churches we could tentatively add St George's in the Castle, which has always been identified as a small crypt-chapel, 28m long by 13m wide, in the old prison (*17a-b*). To judge from St Mary de Castro at Leicester, 48m long by 30m wide overall, and other grand castle churches, it seems far too small and was perhaps a private chapel, the actual St George's standing somewhere else, perhaps near the 'king's house', the second Carmelite Friary, in George Street or Gloucester Green, or even Beaumont Street, all of which may represent orchards and gardens within the castle precinct.

In 1250 there were 19 parish churches, but by 1530 the number had dropped to 13. St George's in the Castle, at one end of the western suburb, was succeeded as parish church in the 1190s by St Thomas the Martyr, newly built at the other end. In the thirteenth century St Budoc's and St John's were torn down and rebuilt on new sites. St Frideswide's parish was abolished in 1298 and the parishioners evicted from the priory church and put in with the small parish of St Edward. The second St Budoc's was given to a group of friars and then torn down, most likely in 1309. St Edward's was joined to St Aldate's in around 1370. In 1427 St Mildred's was pulled down, and the parish added to St Michael at the Northgate by Bishop Fleming who wanted space to set up Lincoln College (p.119). In 1525 the far more ambitious Archbishop Wolsey demolished St Michael at the Southgate and added its parish to St Aldate's to make room for Cardinal College (p.125). In the nineteenth century St Clement's and St Peter's in the Bailey were knocked down and rebuilt on new sites. Between 1891 and 1971 five more parishes were eliminated. In 1891 Merton College took over St John's, the grand chapel, which it had built and shared with the parish for six centuries. In 1896 the city made a gesture of modernity by tearing down its own church, St Martin's at Carfax, to widen the crossroads (*81a-b, colour plate 13a*). In 1961 the second St Peter the Bailey, built in 1874, became the chapel for St Peter's Hall, now St Peter's College, founded in 1928. St Peter in the East, closed in 1965, and All Saints, closed in 1971, became college libraries for St Edmund Hall and Lincoln College. Despite these changes, the Church of England still has eight parish churches in the city centre, four largely medieval, and two partly rebuilt in the nineteenth century, when the other two were almost completely rebuilt.

In the last 50 years there have been excavations at St Peter in the East, a medieval church; at All Saints', rebuilt under Queen Anne; and at St Aldate's, largely Victorian. During the ten years from 1945-55 there was no excavation or observation when the chancel of St Mary the Virgin was damaged by fire in 1946, apart from a hunt for Amy Robsart, nor when the site of old St Clement's church and churchyard was cleared for a traffic roundabout in 1949, nor even when St Michael at the Northgate was burnt out in 1953 and repaired. In 1896, when St Martin's at Carfax was torn down, local amateurs haunted the site, making important but still unpublished records; they recovered Saxon coins and other finds. When its neighbour, St Peter's in the Bailey, was demolished in 1874, nobody looked for finds or recorded the foundations. Casual digging, foundations and sewer-trenches at or near 16 old parish churches have produced a great deal of information; if systematised it might allow us to draw conclusions about their origin, development, architecture and relation to adjacent streets. Burials have been recorded at 14 of the parish churches, enough to show that each had burial-rights and a graveyard until the church was closed, or until 1855, when burials in urban churches and churchyards were forbidden on health grounds. In some towns and cities, like Winchester, parishes had no burial-rights and had to use the vast Cathedral burial-ground. Burials found near other churches but outside the existing churchyards are common enough in medieval towns and imply that the churchyards have been encroached on or altered, or that the churches have been moved. Burials have been found under streets to the west of St Peter in the East and to the north-east of St Mary Magdalen. Near St Mary the Virgin, burials on the other side of School Street (now St Mary's Entry), found to the south-west in 1887 and to the north-west in 1895, show that the churchyard was once more extensive, or perhaps rather that an earlier church stood west of the present church (p.97, *20*). Burials found under Exeter College in 1618, in Brasenose Lane before 1894 and in Turl Street before 1894 and in 1979, show that there was a large burial ground here before the streets were laid out, long before bishop Fleming tore down St Mildred's church. They also show that Brasenose Lane and Turl Street cannot have been part of an 'original' gridded town plan if the churchyard was there first. In this and other matters the parish churches are a puzzling and rewarding study. Loggan's bird's-eye view of Oxford in 1675 shows that St Aldate's, St Ebbe's and St Thomas's had narrow walled churchyards between church and street, while ten other churches rose sheer from the street on at least one side, three of them on two sides. Four churches which stood in a row across the middle of the town had a striking relationship with adjoining streets, seeming to project into them on east or west. St Peter's in the Bailey projected eastward into the general line of New Inn Hall Street, St Martin's eastward into Cornmarket and All Saints' westward into Turl Street, which curves round it, while St Mary the Virgin seems to have been extended over the streets to east and west (*20*).

The medieval churches, namely those of St Giles, St Mary Magdalen, St Mary the Virgin and St Michael at the Northgate, the partly medieval St Cross and St Thomas's and the notably Victorian St Aldate's and St Ebbe's are all well worth visiting. It is not easy to say which of them might claim seniority. The tower of St Michael at the Northgate is the oldest building still standing in Oxford, but St Peter in the East seems to have the most ancient foundations as yet investigated by archaeology. St Aldate's has the oldest datable carved stonework, part of a cross-shaft recently discovered. The earliest artefacts were found at St Martin at

Carfax (p.53, *28a*); while the earliest documentary record of a parish church refers to St Ebbe's and its '*court*' (p.38). St Michael at the Northgate is the most fascinating and interesting of the surviving parish churches, standing on the main shopping street of medieval and modern times. Labels, carefully transcribed, give the text of every wall-monument, and the church's own museum in the tower has a rich and rewarding display, including church plate from All Saints' and St Martin's as well as its own. There is enough information and matter in the church for a volume twice the size of this; and indeed a long-serving vicar, whom I knew well, wrote one, published after his death in 1966. The tower, of about 1000, is a most puzzling structure, hard to understand as a military installation, with two fairly wide north-facing windows at ground level and just above. At this upper level there is a large blocked archway in the south wall, visible on the inside. Did this arch lead into an upper-floor church above the gate and roadway, like the gate-churches at Warwick and Winchester? Did the way out of the late Saxon town lie to the west or east of the tower? Or was St Michael's tower built without military intent at a time when the defences of Oxford lay well to the north (*colour plate 4d*)? With its thirteenth-century chancel and south chapels, fourteenth-century north transept and chapel, and fifteenth-century nave arcades and north aisle, we should try to work out for ourselves how St Michael's was expanded and remodelled. A major alteration was made to accommodate the parishioners of St Mildred's after that church was pulled down in 1427 to make room for Lincoln College, thus doubling the size of the parish at a time when the population and wealth of Oxford were in decline. We can also enjoy Oxford's earliest stained glass, of the thirteenth century; many richly sentimental twentieth-century windows and carved saints set in ancient niches, all painted in modern mock-medieval taste, showing the love and devotion lavished on the church by generations of parishioners. The church was, together with All Saints', an integral part of Lincoln College from the 1420s. Since 1971 it has also been the city church to which the mayor and councillors go robed in ceremonial procession from the Town Hall behind the city mace, the grandest in the country.

St Aldate's was largely rebuilt in 1862, except for some of the aisle walls and the tower, which was rebuilt in 1873-4. In 1960 the church was extended with a range of vestries built on the churchyard to the west, their foundations dug down for 3m through nineteenth-century graves. In 1999 the church was re-floored; many graves and burial vaults were exposed, but little learnt about the building itself. By 1525 the parish, originally of only moderate size with no more than 45 houses, had absorbed another three parishes. The churchyard has seen many changes. In perhaps the thirteenth or fourteenth century the church, or its joint patrons, Abingdon Abbey and St Frideswide's, built houses on narrow strips of land fronting the streets on the east, where the churchyard projected at least 4.5m into the street, and probably also on the north. To the east (*19*) a gold dinar minted at Denia on the east coast of Spain for the Almoravid prince Ali ibn Yusuf in AD 1106/7 was found in 1825 'during the digging of a sewer in the street opposite Christ Church'.

In a medieval Christian context these Arabic gold coins, practically the only source of gold in northern Europe, were used only as diplomatic gifts between monarchs or as offerings at shrines. This strongly suggests that a church on or near the site of St Aldate's held St Frideswide's relics in the early twelfth century. Another gold object, an eleventh-century plaited ring, said to have been 'found about 1890 in a stone coffin in St Aldate's Street, Oxford when excavations were being made for a drain opposite the great gateway of Christ Church', was actually found in 1869 at 31-2 Queen Street 'in an ancient grave, very deep in the ground' and described as 'a very early Celtic Torque-ring of hammered gold'. Was the 1890 'find' caused by sheer muddle, secrecy or dishonesty? This kind of problem is common enough in archaeology.

The splendid medieval church of St Peter in the East, which was closed to become the library of St Edmund Hall, appears twice in Domesday Book in 1086, both as a property of Robert d'Oilli the elder, who held Oxford Castle for William the Conqueror, and as owner of Holywell. D'Oilli's nephew and successor, the younger Robert, may have intended to found a priory here in the 1120s. Much remains of the church of this time, notably a two-bay vaulted chancel above a three-aisled five-bay vaulted crypt of the 1120s. A large property to the west, now part of Queen's College, seems to have belonged to the church. In 1969 a dig revealed a stone church of c.950-1050, an earlier timber church of around 800-950 and, earlier still, post-built huts.

All Saints, another closed church, is now the library of Lincoln College. In 1326 St Frideswide's Priory, which had owned it with eight other Oxford parishes in 1122, sold the church to the bishop of Lincoln. A century later bishop Fleming of Lincoln incorporated it into his new Lincoln College (p.119) and for the next few centuries it remained nominally part of the college but really the parish church for a small and exclusive group of well-to-do citizens. In 1700 the medieval spire collapsed on the church and wrecked it. It was rebuilt in 1706-8, to the design of Henry Aldrich, dean of Christ Church, as a simple rectangular box, like one of Wren's London city churches. Assuming that the road-level would rise, Aldrich raised the floor well above the street, as we can see at the south door, now disused, reached by five steps, 1.2m high, from the street. To make it up to this level, the builders dumped hundreds of tons of rubble from the old church onto its floor, a bit below modern street level, thus avoiding having to cart it away. There was a dig in 1896, when the city council pulled down St Martin's and adopted All Saints as the city church; the interior was rearranged to seat the mayor, aldermen and councillors, and the architect T.G. Jackson reported that:

> On taking up the floor we found a most horrible mess of vaults, graves, and lead coffins, the worst I think I ever saw. Mockford, my clerk of works, was taken ill and it is a wonder the workmen were not all laid up too. I was heartily glad when we had cleared it all out and concreted the floor over.

21 St Peter in the East, crypt window with arch replaced. *Photo, 1968*

Some of the more recent parishioners may still have been liquifying or fermenting under the floor in sealed lead coffins. In 1973 the Oxford Archaeological Excavation Committee excavated the centre of the church, keeping clear of the foundations as the architect and his engineers were convinced that the diggers, working with trowel and shovel, would bring the church down again. In 1974 contractors bulldozed out the deposits along the walls as the archaeologists watched vital information being lost. Under the rubble and vaults, the medieval footing survived in good condition, damaged only by a few medieval burials. Remains of earlier houses were revealed beneath.

St Martin's at Carfax, rebuilt in 1820-2 (*81a*) was pulled down in 1896. Only the tower, perhaps of the late twelfth century (*81b*), is left. All the 'human remains under the portion of the site of the church and of the church-yard thrown into the streets' were dug up and reburied in Holywell Cemetery, the monuments and tombstones being relaid or re-erected at All Saints. The foundations of the north wall, large blocks of Headington stone to a depth of 0.7m, were recognised as work of the 1820s, standing on a rubble footing 0.5m high. This seemed to be fourteenth-century, with fragments of floor- and roof-tiles and re-used stonework. Below this, to a depth of 3m, lay a broad earlier foundation, presumed to be twelfth-century or earlier. Finds included an enamelled bronze roundel of the ninth century (*28a*), a silver penny of Edward the Elder (899-925) and three pennies of his son Athelstan (925-939).

22 St Frideswide's Priory (now Cathedral); *a)* *Above* Interior. *Mackenzie & Le Keux, print, 1832; b)* *Opposite* North–south section. *Cattermole & Le Keux, print, 1820*

Of ten monastic churches in the medieval town only St Frideswide's Priory, now the Cathedral, survives, largely complete (*22a-b, 23a-b*) except for the three western bays of the nave and the west cloister range. Of the other nine monasteries nothing remains above ground. During the last 30 years two friary churches have been excavated and their plans largely recovered, but less is known of their cloister ranges. Between them Oxford's ten monasteries had 15 or 16 different sites, as the Blackfriars had two sites; the Whitefriars had two sites; the Trinitarian Friars had two sites, perhaps both at once; and the Templars moved from Cowley to Sandford. St Frideswide's may have had two sites and St George's may not yet have been found. The two earliest monasteries, St George's, founded in '1074' as a college of secular canons, and St Frideswide's, founded in '1122' as a priory of Augustinian canons, were also parish churches; both foundation-dates are rather unreliable. During the twelfth century the 'monks' or Augustinian canons of St Frideswide's went to

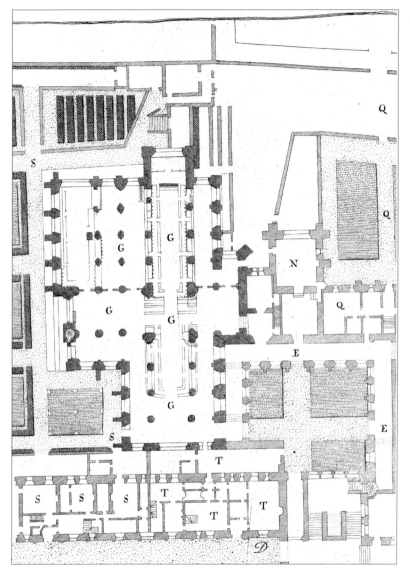

23 St Frideswide's Priory (now Cathedral) *a)* *Above* Plan. *Williams, print, 1733*;
b) *Opposite* Stalls of the 1630s. *Coney, print, 1816*

great pains to create a myth that their church, the present Cathedral, was the nucleus of Oxford and the town's mother church from the 720s. They claimed that their obscure saint, the 'bond of peace' whose relics they held, was a wonderful cure-all for ailments, especially the more revolting skin diseases. Some scholars have naively taken all this as gospel truth, translating, analysing and publishing the twelfth-century legends. But no features or artefacts of middle or late Saxon date, no walls, pits or postholes, no carved stone, cast bronze or even pottery have ever been found at the Cathedral, where constant building-

works, diggings, archaeological observations, restorations and excavations have gone on since the 1850s. The church, cluttered with the trappings of a Cathedral, is the most sophisticated and enjoyable piece of architecture in Oxford, and the most complex and frequently altered structure in the city. It is not all that large, with an internal length of 48m, perhaps originally 61m before Wolsey demolished the three western bays of the nave in 1525-6. Ambitious priors and their patrons, advisers and master-masons made up for the size with a highly original and illusionist design, followed throughout, while they rebuilt an older church in stages between the 1150s and the 1190s or later. This older church, possibly dating from about 1100, may have had a nave of the same length, perhaps without aisles, a shorter chancel, perhaps of three bays with flanking two-bay chapels on each side, and two-bay transepts. Some such plan for an earlier church could explain various anomalies of the present building. Most Romanesque churches, especially early ones of the eleventh century, make a deep spiritual impact, appealing at once through the eye to the heart; but St Frideswide's makes a rather different, more intellectual appeal, through the eye to the brain. Everything about it is structured in distinct levels, and then subjected to a whimsical game in which the levels, however clearly defined in stone, evaporate as you look, but still lead up with a kind of visual logic from one plinth, string-course or line of capitals, to the next. This is quite easy to see as we walk round the church or, better, sit still in one place for service and then walk around quietly afterwards looking and looking again at the whole beautiful fabric from different perspectives.

To appreciate this design and see it in its original state as first built, we have to try to think away the many later alterations in stone and all the later fittings necessary for its use as both a college chapel and also a Cathedral. We must also try to restore, in our mind's eye, the missing west end. The church, like many later medieval colleges, displays advanced architectural fashions influenced by royal taste, not so much that of the Plantagenets as of king David of Scotland, and the styles of the Beauvais region. The church was altered, extended and embellished in medieval times; in the thirteenth century the north chancel aisle was doubled to make the 'Lady Chapel', and doubled again in the fourteenth to make the 'Latin Chapel'. These works may have been meant to provide an ever more ornate setting for the saint's bones, which were transferred to a new shrine in 1289. In the sixteenth century the church saw many changes, which are still not understood, between its suppression as a priory in 1525 and creation as a Cathedral in 1546, having been a derelict building site or at least a condemned and part-demolished building. Between 1546 and 1640 it was repaired; the nave and transept roofs seem to be of that time, and the north aisle may have been rebuilt. In the cloisters we should visit the thirteenth-century chapter house (*colour plate 7f*), where the medieval canons met for formal business. This was designed and built by master-masons from Gloucester Abbey, with fine medieval wall-paintings related to local Oxford manuscript illumination. It houses a display of church plate and the rather tasteless Cathedral shop.

Oseney Abbey (*24*), the grandest building ever built in Oxford with an internal length of 102m, stood well outside the town to the west, on low-lying meadows beyond the castle. It can be compared in size with a fairly small Cathedral, like Hereford or a medium-sized one, like Chichester. The immense Cathedral of Winchester, the longest in Europe, was much larger than Oseney and over two and a half times the length of St Frideswide's at its

24 Oseney Abbey; John Aubrey (1626-97) of Trinity College commissioned the view in 1643 from William Dobson and his assistant, Hesketh; W. Hollar's print in W. Dugdale's *Monasticon* (1673) was copied in 1771 for the *Gentleman's Magazine*; the foundations were quarried away long before that, and the site was ploughed from 1718

longest. Founded as a priory by Robert d'Oilli II in 1129 and given St George's and its endowments in 1149, Oseney became an abbey in 1154. The nave may at first have had a timber ceiling, while the aisles and eastern parts of the church were vaulted. Work on the church, cloisters and subsidiary buildings must have gone on almost continuously from around 1130 to 1190, frequently during the thirteenth century and intermittently until the 1530s, with masons and carpenters based within the abbey precincts, engaged (when they were not needed at Oseney itself), on repair and reconstruction of the abbey's parish churches, farm-property and houses in Oxford and elsewhere, no doubt following house styles favoured by the abbey's master craftsmen. We may assume that the church of the 1130s was extended to suit Oseney's enhanced standing as an abbey. By 1270 it had 11 lesser altars, of which one had been dedicated in 1201, five in 1227, two in 1240, two in 1253, and one in 1263, perhaps as an ambitious master-plan was steadily carried out, no doubt with revisions and changes of plan. The high altar itself, dedicated in 1269 by Richard of Gravesend, bishop of Lincoln (1258-79), was the final stage of an ambitious rebuilding programme, all vaulted like Gravesend's work at Lincoln. In the precinct were almshouses, and retirement apartments for wealthy citizens and public servants, with many workshops and service buildings. In 1542, soon after the abbey was suppressed in 1539, Robert King, the last abbot, was appointed first bishop of Oxford with his Cathedral at Oseney. But in 1546 the bishop's seat was transferred to St Frideswide's and the whole abbey complex earmarked for destruction. In 1565 the walls of most abbey buildings could still be recognised, but by 1578 only the shell of the church was still standing. It was blown up in the 1640s and all the buildings, except for the mill and a long service range, had gone by 1650. Even the foundations were robbed, and by 1718 the site was ploughed; in 1829 the abbey site was a 3ha field let for grazing. The demands of transport and of public health soon sterilised the whole site and put it out of reach of antiquarians and builders alike. In 1845-50 the Great Western Railway built an extension from Oxford to Banbury across the east end of the abbey church; and in 1847 Christ Church sold most of the rest of the field, 1.5ha, containing the site of the church, the cloisters, and probably the abbot's lodging to the south, as a cemetery for city parishes, St Aldate's, St Thomas the Martyr, and St Peter's in the Bailey, the new churches of Holy Trinity and St Frideswide, and another plot for the residents of the Cathedral precincts. Some archaeology may survive under the railway lines and around the modern graves.

From the 1220s to the 1330s a series of religious movements transformed Europe as several orders of friars, called mendicants from their custom of seeking alms, attracted benefactors and built large churches on the outskirts of many towns and cities. The Dominicans or Blackfriars were inspired by Dominic (1170-1221), a Spanish theologian, prior of Osma Cathedral in Castile; the Franciscans or Greyfriars by Francis Bernardone (c.1181-1226), son of a wealthy wool merchant of Assissi, both in c.1205-20. Dominic had made his name preaching in southern France during the blood-stained crusade of 1208-15 to wipe out the heretical Albigensians. After 1215 his followers spread rapidly from the first friary at Toulouse. They focused their attention on universities like Bologna, Paris and Palencia, Dominic's *alma mater* which moved to Salamanca in 1239. Sent by the Dominicans' second general chapter at Bologna, Gilbert de Fresnoy and 12 friars arrived in Oxford on 15 August 1221 to found their first house in England and, (here in particular), influence academic life and thinking. Sworn to poverty and abstinence, without property or endowments, they lived so successfully on charity and begging that, as well as a presence in Eastern Europe, Asia and northern Africa, they had 50 English friaries by 1300, most of them in towns, with spacious naves to serve as preaching halls. In Oxford they soon acquired a group of houses in the parishes of St Edward and St Aldate (just south of Blue Boar Street), handy for their main targets, wealthy merchants to give support, academic theologians to dispute with, and Jewish financiers to convert. These pioneering friars built a chapel and lecture room. The young king Henry III gave them trees from royal forests; and they won support from rich Oxford merchants. Local monasteries like Oseney and St Frideswide's were less supportive when it came to matters like gutters against their property, or parishioners of their churches attending the friary chapel. This earliest friary site in Britain was built over, with no prior excavation or even archaeological observation, in 1966-7 when Christ Church built Blue Boar Quad on the site; the new quad has deep cellars for the college archives only in its north-west corner, so some foundations, floors and other features may survive. By 1237 the Blackfriars decided to move from the town centre to a spacious site on open meadowland to the southwest, bought for them by two generous patrons, Isabel, dowager countess of Oxford and Walter Mauclerc, bishop of Carlisle (1223-46). The friars had to dump vast quantities of landfill to bring the new site above flood-level, only to see the new church subside on weak foundations based on silts and clays. In February 1245, a few months before the new church was complete, the countess died and was temporarily buried in the old chapel. On 1 November 1245 the Blackfriars moved into their new home, taking the countess, in her coffin, to be buried with ceremony in the grand church which she had built for them. Bishop Mauclerc joined them too, resigning from Carlisle and becoming a friar in 1246; he died in 1248.

The friars built a large complex with cloisters and at least three other courtyards. Friary churches were distinctively planned with wide aisled naves for large congregations and long narrow chancels, usually unaisled, for the friars' own use. Between the two parts of the church, in effect two separate churches, was a cross-passage pierced by arches to east and west supporting a tall narrow tower. Built with timber roofs and no vaults, they required little buttressing and could be built quickly and cheaply, but were vulnerable to fire. The Oxford Blackfriars had an aisleless chancel 31m long, very much the same size as that at Greyfriars of the 1240s and at Merton College of c.1280. With its long aisled nave the church, 78m long, was probably complete in 1262 at its consecration by Richard of Gravesend, bishop of Lincoln, who had his own suite of rooms at the Oxford friary and was to consecrate Oseney in 1269. The Blackfriars, most intellectual of the mendicant orders, played the most important role in the development of the university until they were suppressed in 1538. Shortly after that, the wealthy Oxford merchant William Frere tore down the church and almost all the other buildings, apart from a long north-

THE GREAT AND LITTLE OUTER GATE AS WE ENTER INTO REWLEY ABBY.

25 Rewley Abbey; Benjamin Cole, a bookbinder who had worked for Wood, taught himself engraving and published maps and views (*27a*); his rival Burghers (*76*) heard that he planned a map of *Twenty miles around Cambridge* and denounced him to the vice-chancellor in an anonymous letter; Cole then pirated the upper view, of the abbey gates, from one that Burghers had done for Thomas Hearne's *Textus Roffensis* (1720). *Cole, print, 1720*

south range shown on Agas's map of 1578. The site remained as paddocks, orchards, nurseries and market gardens, shown in various forms on successive maps up to 1750. By then the only medieval feature left above ground was part of the gatehouse, which had been re-used as the back wall of a new house built in 1647 at the north end of the site. From the 1820s the city's population grew rapidly and small artisan houses and cottages were built across the area, by then known as St Ebbe's. Hoggar's map of 1850 shows the friary site half built-over. In the 1960s and '70s the city acquired all these houses by compulsory purchase and demolished them for redevelopment. I felt then, and still do, that it was folly to destroy such an attractive quarter of the town. Excavations in 1961, 1966-74 and 1983 revealed the great extent of the friary buildings and some, but not enough, of the plan. The cross-passage between nave and chancel remains inaccessible under a nineteenth-century road. A wide extra bay at the west end of the nave, taken by the excavators to be a later addition, might, however, have been built at the same time as the nave as a narthex or entrance lobby, like a similar feature at Greyfriars.

In 1224 nine Greyfriars, led by Agnellus of Pisa, came to England. Four of them went to London and two of these, both English, came to Oxford where they were welcomed by the newly established Blackfriars, who put them up for a week until they rented a house of their own and began to gather recruits and funds. They acquired several adjacent properties inside the town wall south and west of St Ebbe's church as the nucleus of a site, lying along the southern edge of the second gravel terrace. With generous royal and local support the Greyfriars soon had some buildings put up. In 1245 a patron gave them eight houses and other land outside the town wall next to their existing site within it, and Henry III gave them permission to take down the town wall and replace it with a battlemented precinct wall round the enlarged property. In 1248 he adjusted the permission to allow the north wall of the new church under construction to form the town wall, perhaps hoping that any rebel barons might respect it. In 1959 and 1968-76 excavations revealed most of the plan of this church of the 1240s, much less of the cloister ranges and other buildings, and nothing at all of earlier property boundaries or the earliest friary buildings. The church built in the 1240s may have been simply the later chancel, 30m by 8m, unaisled and perhaps of seven bays like the choir of Merton Chapel, which is almost exactly the same size (50-53). A nave and north aisle, of six bays, were added to the west, and then extended by a further bay; or this bay may have been a narthex built, as at Blackfriars, at the same time as the nave. A stumpy north transept may have been built at the same time as the nave, before being torn down and replaced by a longer transept further west with seven east-facing chapels; later this was to have been extended north by another three bays. The result of ambitious building campaigns over less than a century was a church 74m long, lopsided in plan with an immense north transept 34m by 13m, providing two large preaching halls focused on a single pulpit at the east end of the nave. Transepts of this sort have been found in few other friars' churches in England, but are common in Ireland. As excavated and interpreted the church lacks the cross-passage generally found between the nave and chancel of friaries, often supporting a tall narrow tower. The Greyfriars were suppressed in 1538 and the site sold off in sections and developed with small houses. The church foundations were destroyed in 1969-73 for the Westgate Centre, a dismal mall designed by D. Murray, city architect at the time. The footings of other buildings may survive, robbed in Tudor times and damaged by modern foundations, beneath a multi-storey car-park to the south. Much less is known of the other monasteries.

1 The 'Ox-ford' at the south end of Ferry Hinksey Road. *Photo, 2004*

2 An ornamental gold disc, 'bracteate' or badge of office, from the fifth century AD, found near St Giles' church, *c.*1644. *Photo, 1963*

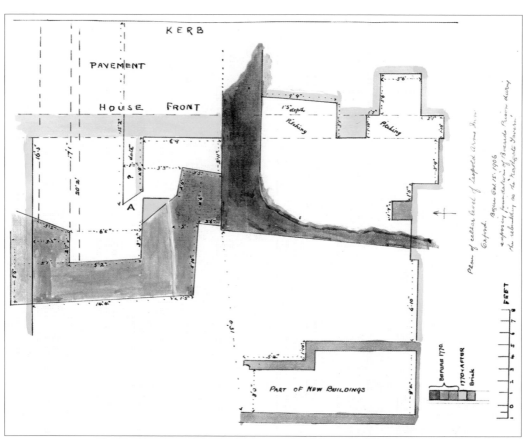

KERB

PAVEMENT

HOUSE FRONT

1'5" depth
Risking

Picking

A

PART OF NEW BUILDINGS

Plan of cellar level of carpeted Arms Inn,
Oxford. Begun Oct 15th, 1906.
exposing foundations of Beaside River during
the rebuilding as the Railgate Tavern.

FEET

BEFORE 1770
1770 & AFTER
Brick

3 Opposite above Archaeological finds between the 'Ox-ford' and the town centre; prehistoric finds are blue, Roman red and Anglo-Saxon green; crosses indicate metalwork, stars indicate coins and large dots burials. In 1883 W.H. White, surveyor to the Local Board, produced the printed base-map, adding the finds by hand; some came from White's 33 mile-long excavation in 1873-80 for the city sewers. When they were finished the city rewarded White with a £1,000 bonus, to the fury of Henry Taunt (*87*)

4a Opposite below Northgate, west gate-tower on P. Manning's plan of the cellar of the Northgate Tavern, 1906; the early footings are black; extensions to the gate-tower green; cellar walls of 1772 yellow; and later brickwork red

4b Right The gabled building, centre, was the Northgate tavern; when the tall domed George Hotel, right, was built in 1910, the ditch was found to be 5.5-6.5m deep

4c Below St Michael's tower (eleventh century), and the former New Inn, (fourteenth century)

4d *Left* Detail of church tower of St Michael at the Northgate, clearly not designed for military use

5 *Below* St Frideswide's Lane, a road-surface of stone and gravel laid in the twelfth century over earlier house-remains, pits and, top, a fire-reddened hearth; note the twelfth-century churchyard wall, right, and high garden wall of about 1550, left, excavated in 1963

6 *Opposite* Research on the Town Wall in Christ Church Meadow by Merton College, 1963: a trench south of the rubble arch (*41*) showed that it did not lead into a drain; auguring indicated a ditch; later we found that it was one of a row of relieving arches

7a-h Medieval and later art

7a *Left* Pastoral staff of William of Wykeham, bishop of Winchester 1367–1404

7b *Below* The third Marquis of Bute (1847–1900), richest of all Christ Church undergraduates, gave a close college friend these dress–studs, ordered from Rowells of 115 High Street

7c *Opposite* 'Monkey Salt', *c.*1500, presented by William Warham, archbishop of Canterbury 1504–32, to New College

7d *Above* Psalter from workshop of William de Brailes in Cat Street (thirteenth century)

7e *Left* Medieval alabaster panel set behind the altar at Yarnton. William Fletcher, banker and antiquary, acquired six of them found near St Peter's in the East in Oxford; and also collected much of the medieval stained glass now in the church

7f *Opposite above:* Corbel head in chapter house of St Frideswide's Priory (now Cathedral), *c.*1260

7g *Opposite below:* The Ashmolean Museum, Oxford, which opened in 1683, displayed a stuffed Dodo, until it fell to bits and was burnt in 1755; a leg and the skull are now on show in the University Museum, Oxford. This Victorian copy of a seventeenth-century Dutch painting of a Dodo is in the Museum of the History of Science (the Ashmolean's original home) in Broad Street, Oxford.

the DoDo & Given by G.Edwards F.R.S. A.D. 1759.

7h Painted glass window
showing Jonah and the
Whale, *c.*1630, Lincoln
College chapel

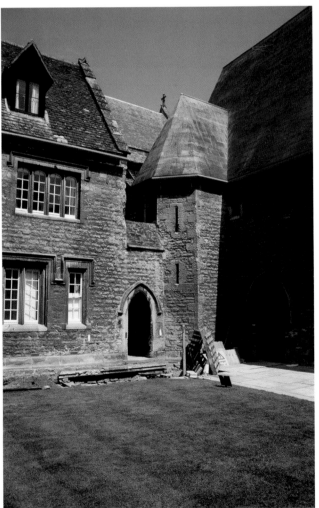

8a-b Top & Above St Mary the Virgin, the university church, from the north, with tower of the 1270s and low two-storey range built in 1320-7 by bishop Cobham of Worcester; the vaulted lower storey was the university's Congregation House or meeting room, the upper storey its first library; and the Old Library roof, originally steep-pitched, rebuilt lower in 1508 with gilt-lead ceiling-bosses

9a-c Medieval colleges: a) Left Merton, the stone-roofed treasury, *c.*1285 and north range of Mob Quad, *c.*1300

9b) *Left* New College dining hall, *c.*1386; the roof was rebuilt in 1863–5 by G.G. Scott; *c*) *Below* Lincoln College dining hall, 1431–37, with its original steep-pitched roof, restored in 1889

10a-b *Above* Memorials of 1635–40:
John and Thomas Lyttelton, drowned in
1635 as undergraduates, monument at
Magdalen chapel carved by Nicholas
Stone; and Robert Burton (1577–1640);
a Warwickshire man, he studied at
Brasenose, taught at Christ Church and
published the *Anatomy of Melancholy*
(1621); he left half his library to the
Bodleian, half to the college, monument
in Cathedral

11a-b Victorian ambition *a) Right*
Meadow Buildings at Christ Church,
built for dean Liddell of Christ Church
in 1862–6; the clerk of works recorded
archaeological discoveries

11*b*) *Opposite* The University Museum, planned by Deane & Woodward of Dublin for Dr Acland's committee and built in 1855-60

12 *Above* Twentieth-century business prestige: an imperial structure at 69-74 St Aldate's (the Crown Courts since 1981), designed by Harry Smith as the centre of Morris Garages' empire, 1932; no boats were found when it was built spanning an old river channel on 155 deep footings.

13a-c Carfax today: *a) Left* View west to St Martin's tower; *b) Below* Detail of tower, with steep-pitched roofline of old church, *c.*1300; *c) Below left* View south-west to corner building of 1931–40 on site of the medieval Swyndlestock Tavern and the Butter Bench of 1710 (*26, 27, 81*); note Tom Tower in the distance. *Photos 2004*

3

THE MEDIEVAL TOWN
1200-1550

During the thirteenth century the merchants of Oxford formed a proud and wealthy corporation, well able to hold their own against the monasteries that ringed the town, and subdue the lesser citizens. They were less successful at coping with an alien trade – the scholars who settled in the town. During the twelfth century the leading citizens had become used to acting together. In 1191 they confirmed the gift of Medley, a farm on the floodplain of the Thames, to Oseney Abbey, which they had made in 1147, with a charter written for them by an Oseney scribe. It looks very like a royal charter and lists, at the end, 62 citizens *Nos Cives Oxenefordie de Communi Civitatis et de Gilda Mercatoris* ('we, citizens of Oxford, of the commune of the city and of the merchant gild'). They authenticated the charter with their common seal, showing their Ox (pp.7, 38, *1*). The seal is round, as kings' and nobles' seals were, quite unlike the pointed oval seals used by prosperous merchants. It reads, round the edge, *SIGILL' COMMUNE OMNIUM CIVIVM CIVITATIS OXENE-FORDIE* – 'the common seal of all the citizens of the city of Oxford'. The town council continued to use the seal on official documents for almost five centuries, until it was broken up in 1662. The seal on this charter of 1191, bought by the city in 1968, is perhaps the earliest example of a municipal seal in the country. It is not clear whether the 'commune of the city' and the 'merchant gild' were once two separate bodies that had merged, or whether the wording is just rather stilted and clumsy. A few years later, in 1199, the leading citizens took a further step towards independence. They paid king John £132 (200 marks) as a lump sum and agreed to pay £63 0s 5d every year to be able to elect their own bosses or 'reeves' and take direct control of their courts, markets, walls, streets, wasteland and some of the mills, which the sheriff of the county had previously controlled as the king's representative. John had just come to the throne at the start of his unpopular and crisis-ridden reign, and in selling the 'fee-farm' of the town he was simply following the example of his father, Henry II, and his brother, Richard I, who had done the same for several towns and cities. A fair amount of myth persists even in the history of civic administration. In the twelfth century the citizens may have gathered in St Martin's churchyard every Monday morning 'to settle local affairs in the Portmoot', as an enterprising scholar book-dealer claimed in 1966. He believed that they had been doing this 'from before the Norman Conquest', quoting a lost land grant, perhaps of 1172, about a property or house-site in an unknown location. In 1929 H.E. Salter had suggested that the townspeople met only once or twice a year in any great numbers. They were writing in an age that believed, without any evidence, in a primitive Germanic democracy and may both be wrong.

In 1229, 30 years after John's sale of the 'fee-farm', his son Henry III, an energetic young ruler, gave a Jewish businessman's house to the 'Burgesses of Oxford', that is the next generation of leading citizens, 'for our courts to be held in that house for ever'. The city still has the actual charter drawn up by the king's chancellor, Ralf Neville, bishop of Chichester, and witnessed by four other bishops, the justiciar and eight other courtiers and officials. It informs us that the house, which had belonged to Moses ben Isaac, lay between the house of Adam the vintner (on the north) and the house of David of Oxford, a wealthy Jewish financier. Examples at Lincoln and Bury St Edmunds suggest that it was a large stone house of the twelfth century with a hall on the upper floor. We can deduce that the property, where the north part of the Town Hall stands today, was 18m wide and rather less than 36m deep.

The thirteenth century was a time of constitutional development when the council, freed from the sheriff's direct control, evolved through a series of phases. At every step the town's richer merchants formed a club within a club to keep inferior tradesmen down and allow them almost no share in their profits. This was common practice everywhere, and in the mid-thirteenth century poorer townsmen at Bury St Edmunds, London and Northampton objected regularly and vociferously. Similar complaints by the lesser craftsmen of Oxford in the 1250s and the 1290s make it clear that town government was geared to making the rich richer and keeping the poor poor, with no nonsense about 'democracy'.

Between 1200 and 1350 the Oxford citizens, as a council, built three impressive stone monuments as symbols of their authority, the Guildhall south of Carfax, the church of St Martin at Carfax, and the Town Wall. They rebuilt ben Isaac's house in the 1250s, and extended it in the 1290s; it was rebuilt again, doubled in size, in the 1750s. In the 1890s they rebuilt it yet again, enlarged still more, as the present Town Hall. Excavations beneath the basement floors should reveal foundations and perhaps parts of the walls and columns of the vaulted crypt of the 1250s (*32a*). Under these remains may be the earlier footings of Moses ben Isaac's house. The merchants met here to organise their attempts, successful for centuries, to keep all other businesses,

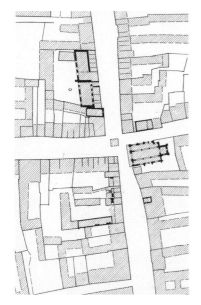

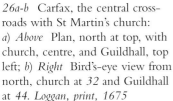

26a-b Carfax, the central cross-roads with St Martin's church:
a) Above Plan, north at top, with church, centre, and Guildhall, top left; *b) Right* Bird's-eye view from north, church at *32* and Guildhall at *44. Loggan, print, 1675*

except for their own, out of the town, and solve their two main problems, to control the 'lesser burgesses' and keep tabs on the subversives who practised that strange and unintelligible trade of buying and selling words. On festive occasions they met at the inns and taverns of their fellow-councillors and aldermen. Carfax Tower, the late twelfth-century bell tower of St Martin's church, where the leading citizens assembled for worship, stands at the very centre of the modern city. The Victorian councillors kept it as a landmark when they widened the crossroads in 1896 by pulling down the church (*26a-d, 27a-b, 81a-b, colour plate 13a-c*), which the earlier councillors had rebuilt in the thirteenth or fourteenth century. Much of the Town Wall survives, defining the area most directly controlled by the council, as a toll-barrier more than anything, thus helping to raise the town's corporate revenue from goods brought in to sell. Its minor functions were to look good and enhance civic prestige, to look imposing as a military deterrent, and lastly to be of some use as a defence, if trouble came. The richer citizens who built it lived in the inner part of the medieval town and based their trading operations there. When they planned the Wall they excluded the suburbs on the west, north, north-east and east, in territory partly or wholly outside their control. Only the south suburb got a special outer bridge-tower to protect it. Outside the Wall the hamlet or suburb of

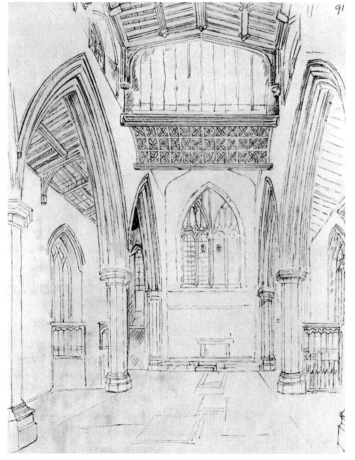

26c-d Carfax, the
central crossroads
with St Martin's
church:
c) Above Church
from south-east.
Hollis, print, c.1819
d) Below church
interior. *Buckler,
drawing, 1819*

27a-b *Opposite*
a) *Above* Carfax,
St Martin's church
and the 'piazza'
from east. *Cole,
print, 1720-1,*
b) *Below* Carfax
area. *G.W.G. Allen,
aerial photo, 1933*

St Martins Church

Quater Vois, alias
Carfax or 4 ways

The Groundplott
of the Conduit

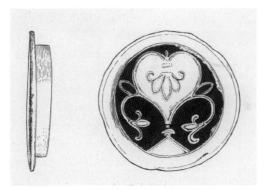

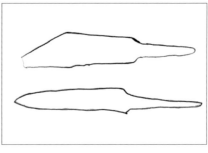

28a-c a) *Above left* Bronze enamelled 'mount' from Carfax church, ninth century; b) *Above* two knives from a drainage-trench in Cornmarket, tenth and eleventh centuries; c) *Left* Stone lamp from Town Hall, twelfth century

Holywell to the north-east belonged to the wealthy rectors of St Peter in the East and, from 1292, to Merton College. Between them they firmly kept the town out of Holywell for most purposes for centuries. Across the Cherwell the outlying suburb of St Clement's was in Bullingdon hundred, under the lords of Headington. It was arbitrarily joined to the city only in 1835 under the Municipal Corporations Act. Residents of the north suburb, the parishes of St Mary Magdalen and St Giles, attended the courts of Northgate hundred, also under the lords of Headington. These two parishes only really became part of Oxford after the city bought the hundred from George Brome for £180 in 1589-92. People living in St Thomas's, the west suburb, could take refuge within the precinct wall of Oseney Abbey, which developed and largely owned the suburb. Attempts to include any of these areas within the Wall would have led to endless disputes; and, as the wealthier townsmen must have asked themselves, why should they defend craftsmen and labourers who paid almost no dues or fees to the town?

In 1226 the young king Henry III or his advisers ordered Gloucester, Oxford and Worcester to attend to their defences, with little effect. From 1227 a combination of special grants and new market taxes induced the citizens to start reconstructing the defences. Between the 1220s and the 1320s they built the Wall in stages on the general line of an earlier turf rampart (p.27, *10*). The leading townsmen most responsible for the work can be named, as they appear in the lists of mayors, bailiffs and aldermen. There were three distinct power groups, one in 1225-40, another in 1245-65 and the third in *c*.1265-95; there was of course some overlap and continuity between the groups, not so much from father to son as through daughters' marriages and widows remarrying. These widows and wives played a major part in the social, political and economic life of the town and also gave generously to local monasteries and to the Hospital of St John (p.84-6). John Pady (d. 1230), leader of the first group, was alderman, not yet an appointment for life, in 1218 and mayor in 1226, 1227, 1229 and 1230. He planned and began to construct the Wall, whether simply responding to royal initiative or by obtaining the first of a long series of 'murage' grants from Henry III. Pady's main associates were Peter Torald, bailiff in 1222 and 1227 and mayor in 1229, 1231-6 and 1240, and Geoffrey of Stockwell, bailiff with Peter Torald in 1222, and bailiff again in 1230, and mayor in 1237, 1238 and 1239. John Pady's aunt Christina, daughter of Ralf Pady, married first the wealthy Laurence Kepeharm, Oxford's first mayor in about 1205, and secondly Jordan Rufus, one of the two bailiffs, (next in seniority after the mayor), in 1227. The original Pady home was perhaps the later Bear Inn (123-4 High Street). In 1229 the king rewarded this group with the gift of ben Isaac's house as their Guildhall (p.66).

Adam Feteplace, leader of the second group, was mayor 14 times between 1244 and 1267; his associates were Geoffrey of Hinksey, bailiff eight times between 1244 and 1267, John of Coleshill, who was bailiff eight times between 1245 and 1266 and mayor in 1269, and Geoffrey Goldsmith, bailiff eight times between 1247 and 1275. They rebuilt the Guildhall in the 1250s, to judge from the architectural detail seen in drawings of around 1750 (*30a-b, 31*). In about 1253 Walter of Milton, one of the *minores burgenses,* presented a formal petition to Henry III, complaining in bad Latin about many details of town government, especially about a group of 15 'jurats' or greater burgesses who shared out the higher offices among themselves, forced all the workmen in the town to join the guild and pay to do so, imposed unjust taxes and so on. He ended by begging the king to set up an enquiry, and gave him a list of 32 'greater burgesses' involved in the whole matter. Adam Feteplace heads the list and Goldsmith, Hinksey and Coleshill come fifth, sixth and seventh. It is not likely that the king, who spent much time at Woodstock and was often in Oxford, paid much attention. Coleshill supplied the king with wine for Woodstock, and also dealt in cloth. Feteplace had extensive business interests in importing wine through Southampton, and large debts owed by Oseney Abbey and the lord of Headington. Always believing in keeping a high profile,

29a-b Grandpont with houses of the south suburb: *a*) *Above* North end looking north with 'Alice's shop' and 'Bishop King's palace'. *Anon, drawing, c.1830; b) Below* South end looking north to Tom Tower. *Carline, etching, 1911*. Both artists exaggerated the width of the narrow road, only 7.3m from house to house at the north end

The old Town Hall in the City of Oxford; towards the Street taken down in the year 1751 & rebuilt in 1752.

30a-b Guildhall, rebuilt in the 1250s. *a) Above* West front with stalls for selling dried or salt fish; *b) Below* Project to remove stalls and restore the 'medieval' form. *Anon, drawings, c.1740*

31 Guildhall part-demolished, with cellar, ground floor, and upper hall. *Green, drawing, 1751*

he had been imprisoned as a young man in 1232 for his part in an attack on students. More than 30 years later, in 1265, the younger Simon de Montfort threw him in prison again until he handed some property over to Guy the armourer, one of Montfort's supporters. To demonstrate his upward mobility, Feteplace set up one of his sons as lord of the manor of North Denchworth in Berkshire, and his grandson fought as a knight in Edward III's army at Crecy in 1346. Forms of town government kept pace with active civic building, and by 1255 there were a mayor, two bailiffs and four aldermen, with another eight burgesses sworn to help them keep the peace and track down criminals and vagabonds. The mayor's position derived from the 'alderman' of the guild, and the bailiffs, the real executive officers, from the sheriff's 'reeves'. The mayor, at first elected for life, became an annually elected officer, and the same happened with the two bailiffs. The four aldermen, formerly changed or alternated, became life-time appointments for the most senior or the richest councillors. The bailiffs' main task was raising money and presiding over courts.

The third group were more closely interrelated by marriage. Nicholas of Kingston, vintner and innkeeper of the Cross Inn, was the town's dominant character from the 1260s. He was bailiff in 1251 and mayor 16 times between

32a-b a) *Above* Guildhall, the medieval vaulted cellar (*31*), often let as wine-tavern, and demolished in 1751. *Drawing* b) *Below* Just to the north, the fourteenth-century vaulted cellar of Knap Hall, built by the vintner John Gibbes (*35*), now the Town Hall plate room. *Drawing*

33 Early footings or stone-lined pit in Mob Quad, Merton College, perhaps twelfth-century, excavated in 1922 and 1992. *Photo, 1992*

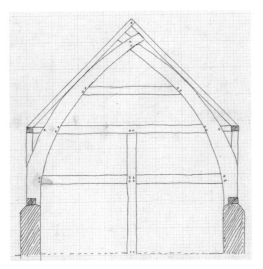 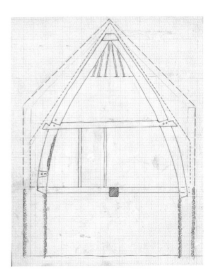

34a-b Cruck houses, *a) Left* 'Near Beaumont Palace'. *Buckler, survey, c.1830*
b) Right Perch Inn at Binsey after fire. *Survey, 1978*

north west view of the ancient building at the corner of Ship Lane, in the Corn Market, Oxford. as it appeared in 1821.

35a-b New Inn, Cornmarket, built by the vintner John Gibbes in 1386. *Above* Buckler, drawing, 1821; he added later discoveries, 1847, 1856 *b)* *Below* dragon-beams at north-east corner after 1950 restoration; note Woolworths, now the Clarendon Centre, in background. *Photo, c.1960*

36 Above Golden
Cross (the Cross Inn) in
Cornmarket, a great
local meeting-place.
Taunt, photo, c.1900

37 Left Northgate,
rebuilt in 1580, from
south with St Michael's
tower and, right, the
former New Inn (*35*).
*Malchair, drawing, 1771;
redrawn for publication,
1788*

1261 and 1284 owning only a few valuable properties near his inn and a few scattered rents from his marriage into the old-established Perle family. Kingston's brother-in-law Henry Owen, also a vintner, was bailiff in 1268 and mayor in 1273, 1279, 1280 and 1292. He seems to have sold the family home in Cornmarket and moved to live on the site of Corpus Christi College; he owned many scattered rents and small properties throughout the town, which his family had picked up over several generations. Kingston's son-in-law Nicholas of Coleshill was the son of Feteplace's associate John of Coleshill, from whom he inherited a good deal of property. He was bailiff twice, and on Kingston's death in 1285 inherited much of his wealth to become the richest man of the town. In 1292 Henry Owen, as mayor, raised a £40 tax or 'loan' and spent it, with further donations from seven other wealthy merchants, on building *communem Aulam eiusdem Villae* ('a common hall for the town'). This was his defence against one particular charge when an aggressive group of less prosperous citizens took all eight of them to court at the Exchequer in London on various charges covering the previous nine years, such as raising a 'murage' tax for work on the Town Wall but not doing the work, and so on. It was very much the same as the petition of 1253. What Owen built at the Guildhall was probably an extra hall at the back, to serve as a committee-room where the wealthy merchants could plot against the humbler tradesmen. The city council still meet, in their late Victorian council chamber, on exactly the same site today. Owen has been accused of being one of 'a ring whose members exercised in turn the functions of office and controlled the admission to the freedom of the borough', very much as Feteplace and his clique had done a generation earlier. From 1306 more junior financial officials, the two chamberlains, began to keep accounts of day to day financial business. The four constables, most junior of the town officials, are first recorded at very much the same time, in 1305.

The Town Wall really needs a separate map and guide to appreciate it fully and to follow it in detail for 2km around the town centre. We can only spare a superficial glance. Starting at its north-western end by the castle, or Nuffield College, we can see, in the grounds of the former Boys' High School in George Street, a length of the Wall and Bastion 1, pierced by a seventeenth-century window. The line of the wall crosses New Inn Hall Street just north of the Wesley Memorial Church and is then concealed behind or within houses built against it in the seventeenth and eighteenth centuries. At the Northgate we find the tower of St Michael at the Northgate, dating from around 1000, which has no visible defensive or military features (*colour plate 4c-d*). Further east, we can just see Bastion 4 from outside Balliol College and another, Bastion 5, by going down a passage beside a sandwich bar. To the east again, the line of the wall is marked by the south wall of the Sheldonian Theatre and by two incised lines on a paved walk east of it. Smithgate was pulled down in 1634, but its former gate-chapel of St Mary (*39a-b*), built or rebuilt in 1520-1 and over-restored in 1931 when Hertford College took it over, stands complete on three levels, a cellar

38a) The old Ship Inn in Ship Street, a terrace of 1762, with four seventeenth-century houses built in pairs, right, backing on to the Town Wall, much altered in the eighteenth and nineteenth centuries. *Taunt, photo, c.1910 b) Below* Plan for rebuilding the inn stables as Baker's warehouse (now the 'Oxford Story'). *F. Codd, architect (85)*, 1881; he kept the medieval Bastion 4, from which the Wall ran south and then east along the backs of the houses *c) Opposite* Bastion 4 from a garden in the ditch to the north. *Delamotte & Jewitt, woodcut, 1837*

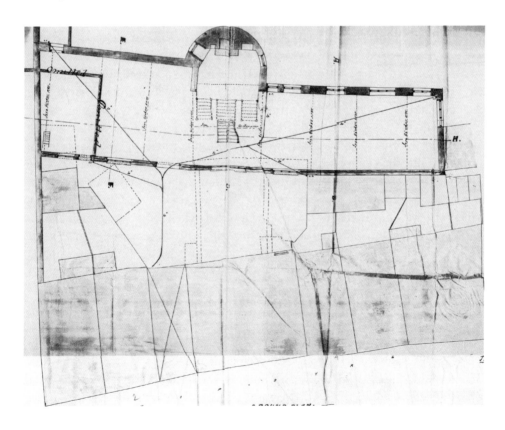

below ground, now a workshop; an undercroft at ground level, now a computer room; and above that the chapel proper, now a student common room. The city leased the chapel out in 1583, and it was a house or shop for 350 years. A 400m length of Wall stands complete in the beautiful gardens of New College, thanks to a shady deal which the town made with the founder of the college, bishop Wykeham, intact and well maintained with six towers, Bastions 11-16. We can see further stretches of the Wall in Christ Church Meadow (*colour plate 6*), and along Brewer Street. The town walls of some cities, London, Chichester, Leicester and Winchester, followed the line of Roman defences and were partly of Roman construction. At Northampton, something of a mirror-town for Oxford, there are two lines, a defensive rampart round an early nucleus about 1.9km long and another, perhaps of the twelfth century, around the much extended 'French' town some 3.8km long. In the fourteenth century Coventry overtook both Oxford and Northampton in prosperity, and its rival twin towns merged and built a Town Wall 3.4km long round most of the suburbs, between 1355 and 1539.

In the 1120s king Henry I founded the Hospital of St Bartholomew in an isolated spot within the royal manor of Headington, 1.7km east of Eastgate. The foundation was for a chaplain and 12 lepers, and the king arranged for them each to get a penny a day for food, with five shillings a year for clothes. This came to £23 0s 5d a year, which was to be paid direct by the sheriff of the county out of the money the town paid for its freedom. The king also gave

39a-b a) Above Octagon Chapel at Smithgate. *Postcard, c.1910 b) Opposite* Section drawn by T.G. Jackson for proposed restoration, *1923* (carried out in 1931 by his son Basil)

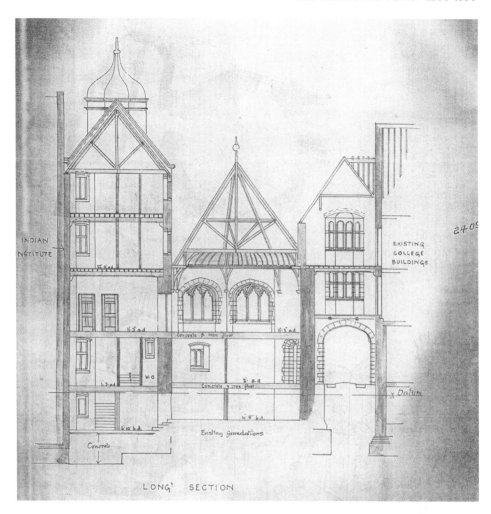

LONG? SECTION

the hospital two loads of hay a year from his meadow on the west side of the town near Oseney. Able-bodied inmates were expected to work on the hospital's own farm or smallholding of 5ha. Over the next two centuries the hospital's income rose by £5 or £7 a year from pious gifts of house-rents in nine parishes in the town, from small patches of wood and farmland in five nearby villages and from six or seven strips of valuable meadowland in Bishopseyt, near Port Meadow in St Giles' parish. In 1316 the number of invalid brothers was reduced to six, looked after by two healthy brothers, a clerk and a priest as master or warden. In 1326 Adam de Brome, founder and first provost of Oriel College, contrived to get himself made warden, with the inevitable result that the college gradually took over the hospital and its endowments. At intervals between the 1390s and the 1890s the city tried to take the college to court, pointing out that the almsmen really should not have to beg in the street while the college let the hospital as an inn or a chemical laboratory. In the end both parties agreed a deal in 1900. One of the hospital buildings, a fine fourteenth-

40a-b Eastgate, as rebuilt in 1711 as a triumphal arch: *a) Above* Inside. *Malchair, drawing, 1771 b) Below* Outside. *Skelton, print, 1821*

century chapel, is still standing, never having fallen entirely out of use, sometimes used for burials. Nearby is a farmhouse of the sixteenth century and a former almshouse with eight sets of rooms, built by Oriel in 1649 after the old hospital was destroyed in the Civil War.

The medieval town had a favourite and very visible charitable enterprise, St John's Hospital, which lasted for more than two and a half centuries, before being seized by a power-crazed bishop as the site for a college. Established by about 1180 outside the Eastgate (its original site is not at all clear), the hospital attracted the patronage of Henry III a few years after he gave the town its Guildhall (p.66). The Jewish community in Oxford, as elsewhere, were under the king's special protection and here they had a 'garden' or burial ground which seems to have been bisected by the road from Eastgate to the Eastbridge. In 1231 the king high-handedly took the northern half of this and gave it to the hospital as the site for a new building. At the same time he seems to have changed its main function from a wayside hostel for travellers to something more like a medical hospital. During the 1230s the king continued to support building projects at both the main Oxford hospitals, St John's and St Bartholomew's, as well as at the Dominican and Franciscan friaries, mostly by giving timber from royal forests nearby. In 1234 he put the hospital on a new footing, with three priests or chaplains, one of them as master, and six lay brothers and six lay sisters to care for the sick. The hospital buildings of this time, the mid-thirteenth century, probably affected the planning of the later Magdalen College in many ways that we do not yet understand, but may discover in the future from geophysical surveys or excavations in advance of putting in drains, service-cables and other such things. The hospital had a spacious site and, behind its buildings, developed a garden to the north. By far the grandest garden in the town, this may have been intended partly for medicinal and partly for recreational use. We can see it today both as earthworks on the ground and also in bird's-eye views of the city by Agas in 1578 and by Loggan in 1675 which show, with some differences, many small formal gardens, orchards, fishponds and plots for other plants. Although the hospital was closed in

41 Town Wall at Merton College, a fourteenth-century relieving arch. *Photo, 1994*

42 Littlegate; the gate was taken down in 1621, but this side-arch for pedestrians survived until 1798. *Skelton, print, 1821*

1457, a century before the earlier of the two maps, we may be confident that they show something of the hospital garden. By 1250 charitable townsmen and women had given the hospital at least 81 house properties or plots in the town. By the 1270s its income from town property was £122 a year; and the hospital remained popular and kept royal patronage, while constantly claiming poverty. In 1293, after the expulsion of the Jews, it acquired their other burial ground, across the road, while evading responsibility for maintaining the road between the two sites.

The setting of medieval Oxford, the farmland around the town, deserves closer study than it has received. Nowadays the Woodstock and Banbury Roads run north for 4.5km through Regency, Victorian, Edwardian and later houses which also line many side streets. In medieval times the town's only north suburb was the absurdly wide street called St Giles. Beside and beyond the suburb, on the well-drained tongue of gravel, the land was laid out as arable and farmed in strips, typical of the medieval landscape, with meadows on the lower-lying floodplains of the Thames and Cherwell to west and east. The strips remained until 1832, a 'medieval three-field system' just north of the city, running north until it met and almost merged with the arable fields of Wolvercote, Cutteslowe and Water Eaton. Every strip of arable can be traced back to 1380, or beyond, just as, sometimes with difficulty, we can follow the ownership of practically every scrap of land in the historic town back to the thirteenth century. A map (*43a*) surveyed in 1769 for St John's College, shows that the strips mostly lay east–west and were roughly organized in five or six long rows from north to south. The three eastern rows stretched north from a stream or ditch on the north boundary of the

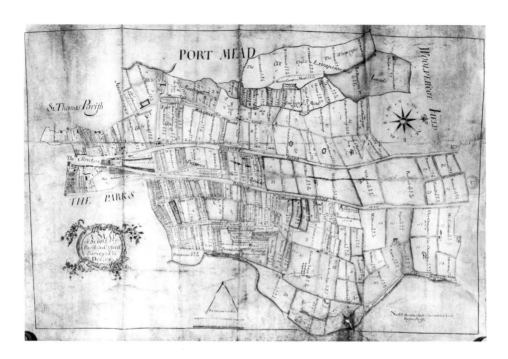

43a-b North of Oxford:
a) *Above* The Open Fields.
*Survey by E.&T. Smith of
Shrivenham, 1769; b) Right* the
enclosed fields. *Plan by J Allen
of Oxford, 1832*

University Parks. The Parks themselves, and all the land down to Holywell Street, formed the separate township of Holywell with its own singular one-field system. In the sixteenth and seventeenth centuries, and probably long before, each property on the north side of Holywell Street had a long strip or field behind it. In 1279 the Hundred Rolls, a great tax-survey compiled for Edward I, listed 24 farms in 'the hundred outside Northgate'. They were small peasant-farms, of 2-21 acres of arable, presumably in strips; three of them had some meadowland. Another survey of the 1380s painstakingly listed 450 strips shared between 21 farms which had from half an acre to 50. This list gives the owners' names in order, furlong by furlong and strip by strip. The West Field lay to the west of the Woodstock Road. The Middle Field lay between the Woodstock and the Banbury Roads. The East Field, larger than the other two put together, lay between the Banbury Road and the Cherwell, or the meadows along the Cherwell. Two wealthy local abbeys, Godstow and Oseney, were the principal landowners from the thirteenth century to the sixteenth. In 1573 St John's College paid Richard Owen £1,567 for his estate in Walton or north Oxford, which included ten farms of 90 to eight acres, most of the former Oseney and Godstow estates. Other colleges, such as Balliol, Lincoln and New College, had also acquired farmland there as parts of other properties in the town. The Survey of 1769 (43a) made nearly four centuries after the written survey of the 1380s, shows 250 strips of arable land, most of which can be precisely identified with those of the 1380s. A lesser farm property belonged to University College from 1360 until 1914, and its history can be traced in the college archives. In the 1240s Geoffrey Goldsmith, one of Adam Feteplace's associates (p.71) who lived on the site of the Covered Market in High Street and was perhaps a kind of banker, began to acquire farmland. A great-grandson added to the farm by buying two adjoining arable strips, now the north side of Little Clarendon Street, some parts of which still belong to the college. The rest of the farm's 15 arable strips, mostly in the East Field, were consolidated in 1832 to form a single block at the corner of Banbury Road and the lane that was to become St Margaret's Road. In 1914 University College sold it to one of the women's colleges, St Hugh's (85), as a spacious site for its new buildings. In the University Parks we can see 'ridge and furrow' remaining from medieval or later ploughing on the manor farm of Holywell. East of Magdalen Bridge similar 'ridge and furrow' remains in South Park from ploughing on the manor farm of St Clements. South of Folly Bridge a very different kind of 'ridge and furrow' can be seen around Eastwyke Farm on the flood-plain of the Thames. This seems to indicate that the low-lying river silts were cultivated in very long strips in an unusually warm dry period, perhaps the twelfth century. Much of Binsey was arable, ploughed in strips for centuries (4). Other parts of the flood-plains, like Port Meadow, remained open and were never divided up by hedges or fences, still less ploughed. Still other parts, like Bishopseyt (now the Trap Grounds), Bulstake Mead (pp.8, 24) and Oseney Mead, were owned in strips and mowed for hay.

4

TALKING: THE UNIVERSITY
1100-1550

For the last eight centuries Oxford's principal industry, the real function of the trade association, guild or 'university' (as they took to calling it) of professional talkers, has been to provide vocational training for bureaucrats and administrators and, less seriously, for aspiring politicians, diplomats, lawyers, journalists and every other kind of actor, as these activities developed into professions, if any of those occupations may be so called. All apparent scholarly, cultural or religious interests are mere camouflage, as Oxford's real business has always been to select and train young minds to argue a case disinterestedly from either point of view, to impose authority by mere words, to divert attention from the obvious truth and never, under any circumstances, to admit liability for anything. Anonymity and obscurity are vital to this wilful delight in obfuscation; myths and legends are to be desired, reality to be concealed. Giving words a new and different meaning has always been enjoyable, and a constant flat denial that higher education is primarily vocational is of course part of the obfuscation game. From the start, all the hack practitioners of talking awarded themselves the title 'master' as if they were the head of their guild, or recognised experts with long training and international experience. In the 1180s and '90s at least three of these real masters were often in Oxford: Elias of Oxford, one of the king's military engineers; John of Bridport, the king's doctor, who was also a king's clerk and rector of the church of St Mary the Virgin; and Amfrid the Physician, perhaps a friend of John's since studying together at the medical school of Salerno in Italy. Although Oxford never developed a school of military engineering, and medicine remained a highly theoretical subject for a very few, these three men may together have played an important role by creating new space for the talkers' guild, to keep it out of the way of other citizens by developing the area of Radcliffe Square and Oriel College in about 1180-90. In 1194 Elias played a real-life part in the legend of Robin Hood after Richard the Lionheart's return from crusade and captivity, when he took his siege-engines north and opened fire on Nottingham Castle, held by adherents of Prince John. He advised on many royal houses and strongholds in the south of England, including the Tower of London, where he worked from 1199 to 1203. He was based at the royal apartments at Oxford (p.43), which he repaired and renovated. At Oxford too Elias may have reported to the king that the north–south rampart and ditch that ran the length of Radcliffe Square and Oriel College could be eliminated from the town defences and sold off, reserving the valuable High Street frontage for his colleague in royal service, John of Bridport, to build a new church (20) to suit the talkers. With his expert knowledge of stonework and carpentry, he may have designed the church.

All accounts of the origin of the university are baffling, complacent and evasive. In 1895 a leading moral philosopher and pioneer historian of universities, unconstrained by a total lack of evidence, argued that a migration from Paris in the late 1160s was the main cause of Oxford developing as a university. He undermined his own case by stating that Paris was not really a university then. In the 1950s a leading archivist-librarian wrote: 'It is now generally agreed that the university has no founder, and that its rise was due to causes which in the twelfth century were operating in other parts of Europe' – which of course is nonsense. Even if there was no single royal or aristocratic patron, the university must have come into being as the result of concerted action by a group, or several groups, of ambitious men of affairs who could attract effective patrons and who all had something to gain from it, but might not wish to make it obvious. They were ambitious, intelligent and determined men on the make who have left many records and clues. Some were interested in hammering Latin into boys' skulls (they called this Grammar) and then training them into using or misusing it for various kinds of arguments (this was Logic and Rhetoric); others, devoted to every known sort of legal argument, became the Faculty of Law; several more, keen on medical knowledge of a theoretical kind, became the never very busy Faculty of Medicine; and one or two, engaged in high-flown fancies about religious matters, became the Faculty of Divinity, and claimed superiority over all the others. In 1984 R.W. Southern, subtle and scholarly, wrote as the first sentence of a multi-volume history by many contributors, all experts at camouflage and concealment: 'The University of Oxford was not created. It emerged after a long period of discontinuous and fitful scholastic activity'. He went on to note the major role that church lawyers may have played as they met frequently at St Mary's for lawsuits about church dues and rights in 1155-95, and suggested that they gave seminars during breaks at the hearings. Five years later he again emphasised that the growth of organised government in the twelfth century required 'many administrators equipped with the sciences necessary for government' and thus stimulated the rise and increasing cohesion of universities at Bologna, Paris and Oxford and, from 1224, the founding of new ones like Naples by monarchs anxious to provide themselves with skilled bureaucrats.

At least we can be sure that in the last years of Henry II (1154-89) and in the reign of his son Richard I (1189-99) a bunch of thrusting misfits and oddballs, as they must have seemed to most citizens of Oxford, started to assemble in the prosperous town. They soon established their own special industry of words, in ways that worked very well for them, less well for their fellow-citizens. These old-established townsmen used their hands to weave cloth or make shoes, if they were craftsmen, or their brains to buy and sell goods, if they were merchants. Accustomed as they were as part of their everyday lives to haggling about price and quality, none of them could see the point of standing about just talking for a living, or probably ever realised what very hard work it can be.

A thirteenth-century scholar, Jordan of Osnaburg, looked on *Sacerdotium, Imperium, Studium,* Priesthood, Government and Learning, as the three pillars of society, or (shifting to another architectural metaphor), the foundations, the walls and the roof of our earthly church, the three virtues which bring to life, increase and rule our spiritual church. The most constant theme of Oxford over many centuries has been the links, often too close, between learning and government, government and learning. Some of the groups of ambitious talkers who called each other 'master' are well documented. In the 1170s the church lawyers John of Cornwall, Gilbert of Northampton, Geoffrey of Llanthony, Osbert of Arundel and Geoffrey of Lardaria were in Oxford for a long court case between the archbishop of York and Guisborough Priory; the judges were the bishop of Chichester and the abbots of Evesham and Forde. In about 1178 Robert Blund, a retainer of the bishop of Lincoln, was rebuked for spending time at lawsuits in Bologna, Paris and Oxford when he should have been working for his bishop. Slightly later Thomas of Marlborough, a monk of Evesham Abbey, wrote that he had been taught law at Oxford in the 1190s by three 'masters', John of Tynemouth, Simon of Sywell, and Honorius of Kent. John joined the household of the archbishop of Canterbury, became a canon of Lincoln and was later archdeacon of Oxford; Simon, a canon of Lincoln, went on to serve the archbishop of Canterbury; and Honorius, who had studied in Paris and written a book on church law, became archdeacon of Richmond and top lawyer for the archbishop of York, the quarrelsome Geoffrey Plantagenet. For these professional talkers who settled here, if only for a time, Oxford had the double advantage of being a very long way from the diocesan bishop at Lincoln, so that he could not easily interfere, but close to the seats of power at Westminster, Windsor, Woodstock or wherever the ever-moving monarchs happened to be or to have left their deputies if they were abroad. They were lucky too in successive archdeacons of Oxford, the bishops' local representatives, who were often themselves former talkers and 'masters': Walter of Coutances, John of Coutances (1186-96), Walter Map (1196 to *c.*1210) and John of Tynemouth, who had taught Thomas of Marlborough (*c.* 1210-21).

44a-c St Mary the Virgin:
a) *Left* Congregation house and library from south; b) *Below* Congregation house; c) *Opposite* Section looking west through congregation house and library; note 'Carnarvon arch', top right, on tower buttress. *Prints, 1837-47*

The church of St Mary the Virgin stands on High Street mid-way between Carfax and Eastgate and attracts more visitors than many of England's lesser cathedrals. This most splendid of the city's parish churches, often called the 'university church', has served since the twelfth century as the university's principal spiritual home, and until the seventeenth century as its main hall for ceremonies and meetings. The two are inseparably linked; the university came into existence in and around the church in the twelfth century and still uses and helps to maintain the church, but does not own it and never has. There is no record of how or when the church came into being (pp.46-7, *20*), just as there is no formal record of precisely when, how or why the university began. The absence of evidence is all the more intriguing as church and parish were, for many centuries, one of the nation's main centres for the spoken, the written and the printed word. School Street, running north from the west door of the church, was the home of the spoken word, while Cat Street, running north from the other end of the church past the east wall of the chancel, was the home of the written word. Old finds allow us to grasp something of the development of the church. In June 1851, while restoring the spire and pinnacles, the Oxford-based artist and architect J.C. Buckler (1793-1894)

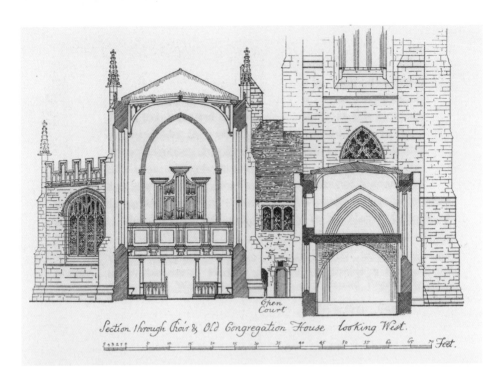

Section through Choir & Old Congregation House looking West.

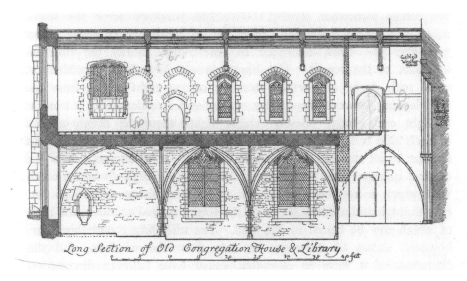

45a-c St Mary the Virgin: *a) Opposite above* Section looking west through chancel, congregation house and library; *b) Opposite below* Congregation house interior; *c) Above* East–west section through congregation house and library. *Jackson, St Mary the Virgin, Oxford, 1897*

investigated the foundations of the chancel north wall and wrote a report for Oriel College, patron of the church. His sketches in the British Library do not give the precise location of the bases and shafts that he found. They were twelfth-century and obviously internal, on the south side of the wall. He must also have dug on the north side of the wall, as he reported that the buttresses, of the fifteenth century, had later foundations than the main wall and needed to be underpinned. A decade later in 1861-2, when the London-based architect G.G. Scott refaced much of the external stonework of the chancel, nave and aisles, he carefully preserved several dozen carved and moulded stones that had been used as rubble in the fifteenth-century walls. By the 1890s, when the next major architect to work at St Mary's, T.G. Jackson, sorted through them, these stones were stored at the Town Hall with much other material intended for a future town museum. He concluded that some were of the late twelfth century, the rest thirteenth century, and he illustrated some of the stones, with dimensions, in his monumental history of the church. They seem to have been discarded by city officials, perhaps as recently as the 1960s. In 1946 the present church was not adequately investigated when the organ caught fire and the chancel roof was almost burnt off, nor the following year when the chancel roof and floor were reconstructed. Enthusiasts dug under the chancel floor in search of Amy Robsart, the secret wife of Queen Elizabeth's favourite, the earl of Leicester, but left no very clear records of their observations. The carved stones found by Scott and studied by Jackson, and the foundations exposed by Buckler, indicate that the twelfth-century church had an aisle-less chancel and, no doubt, a nave; they also show that some building-work was done in the late thirteenth century, whether alteration or extension. To the east the layout of Cat Street with a kink could suggest that the chancel was 5m shorter than the present one. On the west a similar kink in St Mary's Entry, the former School Street, implies that the nave was perhaps 9m short-er than now, a hint supported by the line of the west wall of the Adam de Brome chapel north of the north aisle. By the late thirteenth century there was a north transept at least, as its roof-line is clearly visible on the south side of the tower. The nave may have been aisled with thick round arcade-columns, or it may not; and the aisles may have been wide or narrow; the church may have had a central tower and a south transept, or it may not (20). These are no more than different possibilities, suggestions that would have been anathema to the early 'masters' who knew the church so well, and also to my tutors 50 years ago, who would try to make me argue a case, whether I knew anything about it or not.

Whatever the truth about the early form of the church, it is clear that the university made St Mary's and St Mary's made the medieval and Tudor univer-sity, even though this also borrowed several other churches. St Mary's has a splendid tower and spire built between the 1270s and the 1320s or 1330s, evi-dently with generous support from a princely benefactor or benefactors, form-ing what is still today the tallest building in the city. It must be the result of a long fund-raising drive by successive rectors, or perhaps by the university as principal parishioner. But just as there is no real evidence for the origin of either church or university so there is no record of the donor or donors of the spire. Their identity is another of Oxford's great mysteries, if indeed the ques-tion has ever been asked. The best candidates are Richard earl of Cornwall and nominally 'King of the Romans' (brother of Henry III, the university's chief patron in the thirteenth century) and his son Edmund. Richard was a fabulously wealthy business tycoon with interests in tin, silver, a new coinage. Edmund of Cornwall inherited much of his father's wealth, his estates in and around Oxford, and many of his interests. He founded Rewley Abbey in his father's memory, as a house of studies for Cistercian monks (25). Unlike St Mary's, King's College chapel, a spectacular royal gesture at Cambridge, is well docu-mented as Henry VI's special project, begun in 1441 when he himself laid the foundation stone, and structurally completed in 1515 under Henry VIII. The location of St Mary's tower at the north end of a former north transept is hard to explain. In the 1320s, when the church was still under royal patronage, low flanking buildings (*colour plate 8*) were put up east and west of the tower at very much the time the spire was being completed; whether before, during or after is not clear. The ancient parish of St Mary the Virgin consists of School Street and Cat Street running north, almost parallel, from the east and west end of the church, and Oriel Street and Magpie Lane running south, just across the road from the church. They start on High Street closer together than the other two streets and, as they run south, diverge from each other. Until the nineteenth century the parish also included much of the hamlet of Littlemore 3km to the south-east of the city, with 250ha of farmland.

We can learn more than a bare outline of the life and career of Edmund of Abingdon, an early student and teacher, active in and around St Mary's and in the next parish of St Peter in the East, from papers prepared just after his death, on the way to sainthood. By then he was a celebrated figure, the first doctor of divinity produced by Oxford, the first archbishop of Canterbury to have studied at Oxford and the first saint to have studied at Oxford. A row of houses at the south end of School Street opposite the church, on the site of a possible earlier church (pp.46-7, *20*), was called 'of the fee of St Mary's'. By *c.*1190 master Amfrid the Physician owned the house (i) just west of the north churchyard, where Brasenose College chapel now stands. In *c.*1188 the next house on the south (ii), perhaps a side chapel of the old church, was bought by master Robert of Bukthorpe, presumably Bugthorpe in Yorkshire, an estate of York Minster, to teach Latin, the vital language of international scholarship. At about the age of 12 Edmund and his brother Richard, born in the 1170s as the sons of a devout and prosperous merchant of Abingdon, were sent to school in Oxford 'at the west end of the churchyard of St Mary the Virgin'. He escaped by a miracle when a stone fell from the classroom wall on to the spot where he had been seated a few moments before; the classroom may have been the chancel of the former church. Edmund experienced two further miracles in St Mary's church and another in the nearby fields at a well, now perhaps in the playground of Magdalen College School in Cowley Place. After about seven years studying grammar, Edmund and Richard were sent to Paris for perhaps three years, before being called home for their mother's fatal illness. Edmund put his two sisters into a nunnery and then taught for six years, presumably at Oxford, while saving up his lecture-fees to build 'in the parish where he was then living a chapel in honour of the Blessed Virgin'. This may be the small north chapel at St Peter in the East near St Edmund Hall. The hall presumably stood where he lived during his second spell at Oxford. After further study, perhaps in Paris and at Merton Priory in Surrey, Edmund returned to Oxford, probably in 1214, to become the university's first doctor of divinity. By 1222 he was treasurer of Salisbury Cathedral and rector of Calne in Wiltshire. In 1233 he was elected archbishop of Canterbury, only to quarrel with Henry III and die in exile in 1240. By 1246 he was made a saint; his remains still rest at Pontigny, the Cistercian abbey where he spent his exile.

A vital element in the origin of the university was the need for men able to read and write, as well as count; a second was the medieval Catholic Church, based in Rome; a third was mankind's most compelling product, the book, neither a familiar cheap paperback nor an elegant printed book in hard covers. The book familiar to the medieval scholar was very different. Writing came in several forms, the first a notched stick or scratch or scribble on skin;

not quite writing but most medieval peasants could figure it out. Every peasant who paid rent to his lord's bailiff, in beasts, grain or cash, must have suspi-
ciously watched the bailiff scratching it down, notching it on a tally-stick, or
putting a stroke on a piece of skin. We owe our present Houses of Parliament
to the habit of storing old tally-sticks away. In 1834, a civil servant ordered his
underlings to get rid of piles of them, so they stacked them on a fire and went
home, and the old Palace of Westminster burnt down. The next form of writing was the roll. The bailiff and the lord's clerk had to convert their notches,
scratches or scribbles into names and figures on a single sheet of parchment, a
prepared cow-skin. The clerk wrote each tenant's name, usually in a column
on the left, and then, in a column on the right, the rent paid. He had to add
it up, not easy to do in Roman numerals, with 12 pence to the shilling and 20
shillings to the pound. He then rolled it up and put it in a pigeonhole, to keep
there while it was current, after which it could be thrown into a chest. The
archives of the older colleges contain, between them, thousands of account
rolls; hundreds have been published. Throughout Europe tens of thousands of
these rolls survive in the archives of kings, nobles, archbishops and bishops and
in local record offices. They record rent, building-costs, military call-up numbers, and other things involving numbers. A bright peasant child able to grasp
this slightly ridiculous process might be reported by the bailiff and sent by his
lord to school at the local monastery.

Another use for sheets of parchment, folded not rolled, was as 'charters' or
title-deed of property. Thousands survive among Oxford college archives, kept
as proof of ownership of college property, one or two from the eleventh century, a few dozen from the twelfth, three thousand from the thirteenth, and
fewer from succeeding centuries. Tens of thousands more survive up and down
the country. Very few Oxford scholars ever came across more than a handful
of books, all of which were handmade in every detail and fabulously expensive. Most books available for their use were shabby batches of loose folded-
over sheets, roughly stitched in gatherings or 'fascicules' of eight or sixteen
'folios', or two-sided pages. They could hand these round, or borrow a part at
a time, to copy for themselves, so the outside leaves are always badly rubbed
and worn. In a whole volume, brought together and bound up, you can recognise the separate gatherings. The parchment used for these books has quite
remarkable powers of survival. Scribes also produced books with coloured pictures and words, kept safe within a hard binding, vastly more expensive than
any book today. Library cataloguers and auctioneers call these 'manuscripts',
because they were written, or illuminated, by hand (*colour plate 7d*). These
wonderful old books, often religious works, bibles, psalms and books of devotion, survive in their thousands, loved and protected by the experts who have
devoted their lives to them. We can meet them in Cat Street and Radcliffe
Square, most of all working quietly in the Bodleian Library where they gather for research or to meet. We can sometimes overhear their esoteric

46 Merton Street: Beam Hall with, far right, Postmasters Hall; both probably of the twelfth–thirteenth century, with seventeenth-century gables. T.G. Jackson's Corpus Christi annexe of 1884-5, left, replaced 'The Pit', another early hall. *Taunt, photo, c.1900*

discussions in the Kings Arms. It is only slightly easier to understand people who know all about printed books. I know more about holes and trenches, examining buildings and bookcases, so I can sometimes understand parts of these conversations. Between the thirteenth and fifteenth centuries, before printing was invented, every one of the dozen or so houses on either side of Cat Street was often the home and shop of a parchmenter, scribe, illuminator or bookbinder, all craftsmen who made hand-written books by hand using the most arduous, technical and difficult skills of the day. The parchmenters scraped skins down and soaked them in alum and other substances, cut them to shape and folded them. The scribes, with some less adept helpers, made ink from oak galls, cut pens from quills and ruled lines on the prepared skins (or parchment, as they called it), not at all an easy task with such an intransigent natural substance. The skilled scribes wrote on the skins, leaving gaps for coloured letters and pictures. The illuminators drew pictures in the gaps and added colour to the letters, first sketching the outlines and then colouring them in. The bookbinders sewed the skins together in gatherings and then sewed the gatherings on to linen strips. To keep the whole contrivance together they fastened the linen strips to thin sheets of wood, on to which they glued leather to protect the end-products, which were now becoming books.

47a-b Tackleys Inn, 106-7 High Street; a large double-pile thirteenth-century building, the first home of Oriel College in 1326: *Above a)* Rear with tall hall window. *Photo, 1975; b) Opposite above* Shops on High Street front and, left, Oriel's Rhodes Building, 1908-11. *Taunt, photo, c.1911*

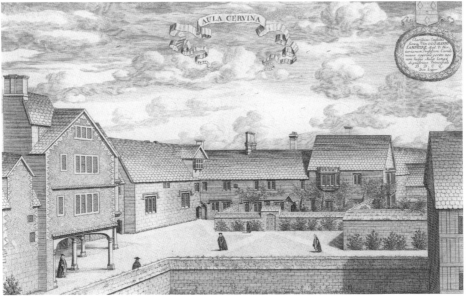

48 Hart Hall, an academic hall bought in 1312 by bishop Stapeldon of Exeter, the first home of Exeter College, which in 1378-86 rented it to New College, then being built; it reverted to an academic hall until Richard Newton, principal 1710-53, raised it to become Hertford College in 1740; this failed and was taken over and partly rebuilt by Magdalen College to house its near neighbour Magdalen Hall, another academic hall. This became the second Hertford College in 1874. *Loggan, print, 1675*

From the twelfth century binders often stamped the leather covers with decorative motifs which, we are told, had nothing to do with the invention of printing in the fifteenth century. All these craftsmen, several dozen at every service, worshipped in their church of St Mary the Virgin. Graduate scholars or lawyers hired teaching-rooms or 'schools' in School Street, now the west side of Radcliffe Square, and haunted the scribes and bookbinders of Cat Street, now the other side of the square.

To keep their industry going the talkers required a constant flow of people to talk at. They had all paid to listen to previous generations of talkers. To make a living, they had to attract and keep future generations listening and, by doing so, learn how to talk. This involved finding accommodation for themselves and providing it for the new students in large houses. These early academic halls include a group on the north side of Merton Street, several of which are of around 1200, and another, Tackleys Inn, of the late thirteenth century. (46-47).

5

THE MEDIEVAL COLLEGES
1250-1550

Most visitors come to Oxford to see the colleges, so permanent and prosperous, their impressive gate-towers leading to grand stone buildings and gardens, or at least allowing glimpses of them. They go away bemused, puzzling over the links between knowledge and the great architectural display that they have marvelled at, wondering what this historic centre of learning, now such a showpiece, was really like in the past. The colleges jostle each other for space around their own secret paradises at the heart of the city, as if they had been there before anything else, whether defences, markets or workshops. In much the same way, wherever a medieval king halted and set up court, at Woodstock, Windsor or Westminster, his bishops and lesser clerics, well aware that the pen is mightier than the sword, jostled both the great earls and barons who were supposed to advise the king on military matters and supply his troops, or at least raise money for them, and also the great merchants who lent the king the money he needed. They were the essential royal administrators who knew about finance and were also the churchmen, who perpetuated their names and duty to the state by founding colleges. In those days no one dreamed of keeping religion out of politics, or politics out of religion; the two belonged inseparably together, as part of running the country. Time spent at Oxford could lead to a career as a king's clerk, for men with a knack of seeming to get things done. In a classic medieval success-story, this was followed by appointments to rectories, archdeaconries and canonries. Regardless of his spiritual or pastoral gifts, any succesful public servant, during or after a time as chancellor or treasurer could expect to be made a bishop or even archbishop.

As we walk up and down the streets, stopping to read the forbidding notices at the college gates, we realise that each of these secret worlds has a distinctive character, established long ago. Each is a monument to ruthlessness, money and duty, left by a powerful and wealthy bishop or ambitious priest determined to leave his mark on his own and later times. They were not devout and holy men, but hard-working, hyperactive, ruthlessly competitive officials working for our medieval kings. Rewarded with top jobs in the church, in lieu of index-linked inflation-proof pensions, some of them founded colleges to produce more people like themselves. Ambitious statesmen have tried to reform these resilient and thriving institutions without much success, in the 1550s, 1650s, 1730s and 1850s. Even in the twenty-first century resentful politicians seem intent on reforming the colleges. Of 12 remaining medieval colleges, seven were founded before 1400 and five between 1400 and 1540, all for slightly different reasons. At first only a few took younger students; now they all do, except All Souls which supports only graduates, the original function of them all. Each college is a kind of independent republic with its own traditions, a theatre for its fellows and undergraduates. In their early days colleges were not as permanent as they seem. Several began, not on their present site, but somewhere else in Oxford, often in temporary accommodation (*48*). Merton, wealthiest of the early colleges (*52*), was not a self-governing body in Oxford but was run from a large estate far away in Surrey. Exeter College had no control over its original endowment in Cornwall; the income was simply paid over by the Cathedral authorities at Exeter. With masterly hypocrisy and great acting ability all the old colleges put on impressive displays of military might, dressing up as castles and making a show of shields. Battlements, useless on a place of learning, were once special to the warrior class; no magnate or knight dared to put up battlements on his castle or manor gatehouse without a 'licence to crenellate' from the king. Elaborately painted shields or 'coats of arms', lavishly strewn around the colleges, part of the secret, half-forgotten language of heraldry, remind us of founders, patrons and benefactors. Covered in armour from head to toe, a great lord could be recognised by his personal colours on his shield and banner. Three red chevrons on a gold background (or *three chevrons gules*) instantly identified that great troublemaker Gilbert de Clare (1243-95), ninth earl of Clare, eighth earl of Gloucester, seventh earl of Hertford, lord of Glamorgan and much of south Wales, as he rode into battle against his own king, his English neighbours or the Welsh whose land he seized to build the greatest of private castles at Caerphilly. One of his tenants, a priest called Walter, a clever cook's son from Basingstoke, had no arms of his own when he leased an estate in Surrey from earl Gilbert, so he adopted the Clare arms, changing the colours to make each alternate half-chevron blue (*or three chevrons countercharged per pale azure and gules*). Starting as a land agent for the Augustinian priory of Merton in Surrey, Walter decided to call himself 'de Merton' after the priory. After a few years as a royal clerk, he went north to Durham to work for bishop Nicholas Farnham for five or six years in the 1240s before returning to royal service at a time of unrest and occasional civil war. He held the highest office of state as chancellor of England in 1261-3 and 1272-4, well aware, in those unsettled times, that it might not last. By 1262 he was supporting students at Oxford, where he may have studied, and in 1264 he made a legal settlement for his students. Before he died as bishop of Rochester in 1277, Walter had established a college at Oxford, naming it Merton rather than Basingstoke. Neither the bishop nor his college ever had to carry a shield into battle, but his college has for seven centuries displayed his special version of the Clare arms, to pay homage to 'Red Gilbert' and lay claim to the protection and patronage of his family, even though the last of the Clares, Gilbert's son, fell at Bannockburn in 1314.

All over Europe colleges for learning were founded at universities like Aberdeen, Angers, Avignon, Bologna, Padua, Prague, St Andrews, Salamanca and Toulouse in 1250-1500. The largest group, of more than 40, was in the great university city of Paris, where none survives; the name of one, Sorbonne, founded in 1257, has become shorthand for the whole university. As well as these, many less learned colleges were founded in Europe, often at the burial-church of a great noble family. In England about 200 such colleges were established in 1260-1500, reviving a much older pattern of Anglo-Saxon minsters. As in the universities, bishops took the lead, typically in remote areas. In 1264 bishop Bronescombe of Exeter established a group of priests at Glasney in Cornwall, increasing their endowments in 1275. Antony Bek, bishop of Durham 1283-1311, founded three, at Bishop Auckland, Chester le Street and Lanchester, and a fourth at Howden, on outlying Yorkshire lands of his bishopric. Other bishops and archbishops followed their example, and the king copied them. In 1348 Edward III established a college at the palace chapel in Westminster which Edward I had begun in 1292. Nobles and wealthy knights soon realised that priests organised in this way would be handy for the office-work of their estates, as well as praying for the noble patrons and their families. Many colleges were founded in 1330-50; many more in 1380-1430. They came in various forms but can often be recognised by a grand chancel attached to an ordinary country church. Some still have a residential range or courtyard near the church, often now a farmhouse.

Oxford's medieval colleges of 1250-1550 carry in their architecture a series of coded messages. A brief glance at the outside of a building, or at one of Loggan's views of 1675 (52), tells us a great deal about the interior. In a tall range, a row of three to eight large windows means 'dining hall' and a row of bigger windows means 'chapel'. Ranges of rooms for fellows and students always have a mixed pattern of two-light windows, indicating the shared bedroom/living-rooms, and single-light windows for the small private studies partitioned off in the corners. A row of two-light windows (or single-light on the oldest, like Merton) means 'library'. An odd-looking square building in a corner near the dining hall will be the 'kitchen' and so on for latrines, wells, pumps. We can learn a lot about the rooms from chimneys on old views. One tall octagonal stack is likely to be medieval, heating an upper-floor room. Three rectangular stacks side by side must have been inserted in the seventeenth century to heat rooms on the ground floor, the upper floor and a new attic in the roofspace.

49 Left Merton College,
hall door and doorway,
*c.*1270. *Print, 1847*

We will look at five medieval colleges, the oldest, Merton, of the thirteenth century; the most thoroughly destroyed, Canterbury, of the fourteenth century; the smallest, Lincoln, of the fifteenth century; the most pretentious, Magdalen, also of the fifteenth century; and the grandest, Cardinal, of the sixteenth century. Merton, Lincoln and Magdalen still flourish. Canterbury and Cardinal were swallowed up by Christ Church in 1546. Nothing survives above ground of any of the early colleges except at Merton, the college of the three chevrons, which has seven or eight fine stone buildings of 1270-1380. They all deserve the closest examination, from the dining hall of the early 1270s and the chapel planned soon after to the library of 1373-8. Like all manor houses and palaces of the time, Merton is a haphazard unplanned complex, and its rich archives contain hundreds of records. Eminent Mertonians worked through them in the 1660s, 1850s, 1880s, 1930s and 1960s to produce a coherent story, glossing over many uncertainties. Despite the wealth of documents and architecture, there is still much to discover. The main site of the college, on the south side of Merton Street (formerly St John Street), is long, 250m along the street, but quite shallow, no more than 80m from the street to the Town Wall (*49*). There were 15 house properties on the street, probably all of them occupied in the town's prosperous and populous days in the 1260s, when the college started to take them over; but part of the site had been meadow or marshland, reclaimed perhaps in stages in *c*.1180–1330. The college began at the west end of the street in four adjacent houses which Walter de Merton bought in 1266–8 to house the students whom he had been supporting. In January 1266 he bought the parish church of St John the Baptist and a plot which went with it from Reading Abbey; but he had to wait until the rector, William Chetyngton, died in 1292. Next door to the east, Merton bought two houses in 1267, one of which had sitting tenants for the next three years. Anthony and Thomas Bek, brothers, were to become bishops of Durham (founding four colleges in the north) and St David's. In 1268 Merton bought the house next door but one. Despite centuries of study, the exact location of the houses and even of the church is far from clear. A notion that the church lay on the north side of Mob Quad, south of the college chapel, disregarded the way all parish churches in Oxford stood on the street, but excavations on this site in 1922 and 1992 revealed, not burials or church-walls, but house-walls of the twelfth century (*33*), running at an odd alignment which suggests that the whole area was drastically replanned, perhaps in *c*.1190, when Merton Street itself and all the properties in it may have been laid out. The old parish church may one day come to light under the churchyard or north transept of the chapel and prove to have been founded in *c*.1190 too. One of Merton's special unsolved problems is the date of the chapel, which for centuries served both a rich college and a small parish and still remains unfinished, with south transept of the 1360s, north transept of the 1420s, a splendid ornate tower of 1448–50, and no nave (*50* and *51*). The chancel, seven bays long and as grand as a friary church, must have

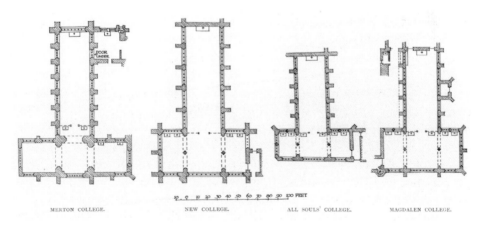

MERTON COLLEGE.   NEW COLLEGE.   ALL SOULS' COLLEGE.   MAGDALEN COLLEGE.

50 Plans of college chapels; left, Merton and New College (both unfinished); right, All Souls & Magdalen (both designed, in the fifteenth century, to copy them). *Vallance*, Old Colleges of Oxford, *1912*

MERT°N COLLEGE.
OXFORD
SKETCH ELEVATI°N.
OF THE WEST END
OF THE CHAPEL

51 Merton chapel, west front, showing marks of proposed or demolished nave and ailses. *Vallance,* Old Colleges of Oxford, *1912*

been built between 1275 and 1300, but the records are no use in finding a more exact date: in 1845 one scholar found evidence of 'the dedication of the high altar in 1277, proving that the work was then sufficiently advanced to allow of services'; in 1954 another wrote, optimistically, that the 'accounts resolve most of our difficulties. Work upon the choir of the church began in the summer of 1290. By the summer of 1294 it was in effect completed'; in 1964 yet another noted that 'The new chapel was being fitted out in 1291'. Its close similarity with work at Exeter Cathedral suggests that the chancel dates from *c.*1275-85, with crossing arches added in the 1290s, perhaps capped by a low tower and opening into shallow transepts, like a friary church. The foundations of a spacious nave, five or six bays long, may have been laid in the

52 Merton College from the north with, bottom right, thirteenth-century drain and top left, Fellows Quadrangle of 1608-10 (p.151). *Loggan, print, 1675*

53 Merton chapel interior. *Skelton, print, 1817, pirated from Turner & Basire, print, 1802*

1290s and its arcades and aisle walls at least partly completed by the 1330s. Two or three bays may have been roofed for parish use; but, perhaps in the 1340s, this nave may have cracked and even collapsed as the footings subsided into the silts of a forgotten stream-bed, leaving the parish homeless and the low tower unsupported. Over the next two generations this disaster, as I suppose it to have been, led to lavish repairs and the building of the present spacious transepts, founded on natural gravel. The chapel was solemnly reconsecrated on 6 November 1425, probably much as it is now, but without the tower.

Hidden away within Merton, Mob Quad is Oxford's oldest and smallest medieval quadrangle (19.7m by 20m), deeply satisfying to the eye, and to the brain too in that it rewards close structural analysis, with details that take us to Persia, south-east France and north Wales. It was not planned, but built rather haphazardly in three main phases. The north range was dated to '1304-7' and hailed as an adaptation or replacement of the old parish church by H.W. Garrod (1878-1960), fellow of the college, Latinist, expert on Keats and professor of poetry. In 1922 he dug at the east end of the range, finding walls that he recognised as an 'anchorite's cell' attached to the church. I walked through the quad on a summer Friday in 1992 and was amazed to find his excavation open (*33*); Garrod had had it bricked round and capped over with girders and concrete slabs, which had been taken up that day for repaving. The bursar was in his office and at once gave me permission to investigate further, so I spent the Saturday and Sunday cleaning up and plotting the old foundations, as Garrod seems not to have left a plan; I dug a tiny trench beside it, like a bit of 'keyhole surgery'. This north range, like the rest of the quad, has its original roof-timbers and floor-beams which should one day give an exact 'tree-ring date'. The east range, including the treasury at the north-east corner (*54*), is all of the same period; the coursed rubble stonework runs continuously all the way along, though most of the windows and some of the doorways are later insertions, like those of the north range, of the fourteenth or fifteenth centuries. Two different bits of evidence demand a date in the mid or late 1280s: between October 1288 and February 1289 'master' Hamund Lincoln, bursar, accounted for fourpence paid to make grills for the treasury windows. This may have been a final instalment paid for work done a few years earlier, but we can narrow the date down on other grounds. Two of the treasury windows are distinctive 'Carnarvon arches', common on the former lands of the counts of Savoy in south-eastern France and western Switzerland and also on the great castles that Edward I built in north Wales in the 1280s with craftsmen summoned from every county. Count Philip lent the king, his great-nephew, his chief military engineer, Master James of St George to build those domineering castles. James imposed his own quirky techniques to speed things up on the hundreds of masons assembled at Conwy to build castles. A pointed arch, however narrow, needs a carpenter for timber centreing, whereas 'Carnarvon arches', with corbelled shoulders and a flat top can be built without. We can see

54a-c Above & overleaf Merton College, treasury of *c.*1285, exterior, plan and interior. *Prints, c.1850 (See colour plate 9a)*

them 20km south-east of Lyons at St-Georges-d'Espéranche, the castle from which Master James took his name. He and his assistants trained the masons sent to Wales, one of whom returned to build these arches at Merton, and also St Mary's where they can be seen (*44c*). The third phase of Mob Quad, built in 1373-8 if the rubbed and illegible building-accounts may be trusted, is the south and west ranges, still used for reading archives, manuscripts and early books and, on the upper floor, the old library, now something of a showpiece. Documents, the details of stonework and roof-timbers, and archaeology all make it clear that this was not a completely new building, but partly recycled.

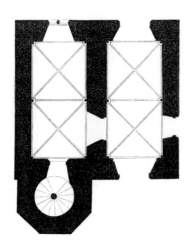

55 School of Pythagoras or 'Stone House' at Cambridge, large stone house of *c.*1190-1200; bought by Walter de Merton in 1271 for income or as a bolt-hole for his college, if Oxford turned out to be a mistake. *Buck, print, 1730*

In 1338 the college discussed repairs to a previous library, which was lime-washed and repaired in 1346 and 1349. This older library was built in about 1310-25, to judge from 16 identical single-light windows in the outer walls of the present L-shaped library, which closely resemble the original windows of the old library at St Mary's built in the 1320s by bishop Thomas Cobham (*44a*). Both sets of windows have elegant ogee heads and simple cusping derived from art-objects brought in the 1290s by envoys from Persia to the court of Edward I. The previous library, then some 50 years old, must have been dismantled and its windows re-used, while the north and east windows of the library are very different, with two-centred cinquefoiled heads, typical early Perpendicular domestic work suiting a date of around 1375. Each set of windows has an odd one out, which readers must find and explain for them-selves. The roof-timbers seem to include many recycled trusses, and 'tree-ring' dating might give dates of *c.*1320 and *c.*1375. In 1995 I was able to make two more tiny excavations in advance of more repaving, and found evidence for an older library at the south-west corner of the present one. Three courses of off-set rubble foundation forming a corner, bedded on natural gravel, lie beneath three rubble foundation-courses of the present library, but at a very different angle, anti-clockwise by some 15°. The first library, taken down and re-aligned after only half a century, may have run northward from this corner, or east-ward. If it ran north, it could have been damaged in my putative collapse of the nave or in the dismantling of the first tower and south transept; or it may have looked awkward, projecting from a newly enlarged south transept rebuilt in '1367-8'. If the old library ran east from this corner, it may have made the north and east ranges of the quad, at a different angle, look odd. The library of the 1370s created a regular courtyard with four right-angled corners, the first in any academic college, at the cost of deep and costly foundation-works.

56a-b Canterbury College, founded in 1363 by archbishop Islip of Canterbury partly as a house of study for his Cathedral monks, later part of Christ Church: *a) Opposite* From the west. *Loggan, print, 1675*; *b) Above* Gateway, demolished in 1775, from the east. *Malchair & Jenner, etching, 1793*

57 New College (founded by bishop Wykeham of Winchester between 1369 and 1386, when the college moved from Hart Hall *(48)* to take over the completed college), with all its members in hierarchical order. *Drawing, c.1460*

My other small dig, at the south-east corner of the library in 1995, showed that the master-mason William Humbervyle had to dig into marshy silts to lay very deep foundations linked with relieving arches, and thus be able to square off the new quadrangle. Merton, like three more of the earliest colleges, University College, Balliol and Durham (now Trinity), had close links with the prince-bishops who reigned at Durham in the far north. We should briefly note that in 1270 Walter de Merton bought a large stone house in Cambridge (55) on a large plot next to the river with extensive arable strips in the fields; presumably he was planning a bolt-hole for his students if Oxford turned sour or the university failed.

In 1361 a former fellow of Merton decided to found a college at the west end of Merton Street. Simon Islip (c.1285-1366), archbishop of Canterbury from 1349, established Canterbury College in 1363. The monks of his Cathedral priory may have sent some of their number to study at Oxford from the 1270s, as they did to Paris in around 1285-1310. In the 1330s and '40s the Cathedral authorities hired a hall by the church of St Peter in the East to house a handful of student-monks, and later they acquired rooms for them in Gloucester College, the main Benedictine house of study at Oxford. After his time at Merton, Islip had been secretary to Edward III and ambassador to France. He seems to have had two objectives, to maintain a supply of parish priests at a time of economic crisis after the Black Death, and to give the monks a place to study, as the monks of Durham Cathedral had had since the 1280s. During Islip's last illness in 1365, the monks were expelled and, after much legal dispute, they were re-established in 1370-3 with full control of the college. In c.1370-1440 they built an entire quadrangle in stages (56a), adding a library projecting to the west in c.1450. With the town now in decay they were able to acquire a site, closer to the centre than Merton and much larger than they needed, of some 24 properties between St Frideswide's churchyard and Bear Lane in the north. In 1540 both Canterbury Cathedral and its college were suppressed. In 1546 Henry VIII handed the college site and buildings to Christ Church, his newly refounded Oxford college. Prints and drawings show what it was like, with a low arched entrance on the east, facing down Merton Street; the chapel in the south range, and the hall on the west, opposite the entrance (56a-b). The last part of Canterbury College, the south range, was torn down in the 1780s, so that nothing remains above ground. Even the foundations may have been grubbed up to re-use the rubble for the eighteenth-century Canterbury Quadrangle.

In 1427 Richard Fleming (c.1375-1431), bishop of Lincoln from 1419, started to found Lincoln College, giving it a charter in 1429. As a young priest he had the bad luck to get on the wrong side of one of Islip's successors at Canterbury, Thomas Arundel (1352-1414), archbishop from 1396, who accused him of sympathising with John Wyclif, who thought that ordinary people should be able to understand scripture in their own language and make

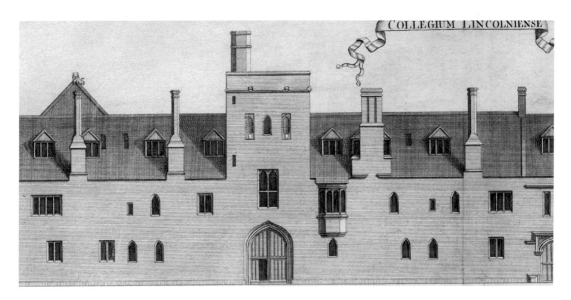

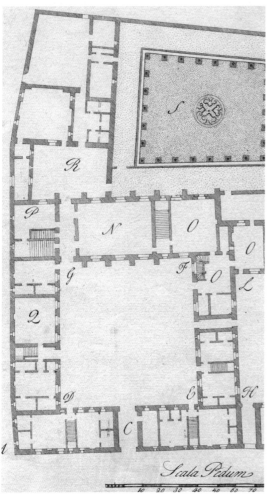

58 Lincoln College, founded in 1427 by
Richard Fleming, bishop of Lincoln. *Plan
and elevation from W. William's* Oxonia
Depicta, *1733*

out what was going on in church. He soon learnt better, gave up all those ideas and, as bishop, had the heretic's bones dug up, burnt and thrown in the river. His college, barely begun before he died, was meant to be, like the university's Divinity School, a symbol of orthodox belief. He intended it for a rector, seven fellows supposed to be studying theology for work in the diocese and two chaplains and had begun to build on the site, the parish church of St Mildred (p.50) and several houses or academic halls. The bishop had good friends like John Forest, dean of Wells, who built much of the Front Quad; measuring 22.5m by 21.5m, this makes it the smallest of the medieval colleges (*58*). Other clerics and local citizens have always been generous to this most unpretentious of colleges. By 1440 Lincoln had a west range with gate-tower where, perhaps, the rector had a room or two; a north range with library and chapel on the upper floor, and an east range with a splendid dining hall (*colour plate 9c*) with kitchen behind and rector's lodging to the south. Except for part of the north range, Lincoln still has all its original roofs, which might provide more precise 'tree-ring dates' for the college buildings. The ten or so members of the college can only have used the hall on special occasions with important guests. They probably ate most of their dinners in a rather grand room with a splendid roof, over the pantry and buttery. No one can appreciate this properly because much is concealed behind later partitions and student rooms in the roof-space. The fifteenth-century rooms in the west and north ranges pose a special Lincoln puzzle: why were they built with two, three or four little studies, as if the well-subsided fellows would have to take lodgers, students or servitors?

Three bishops of Winchester, which was reputedly the wealthiest of all European bishoprics, founded colleges, William of Wykeham at New College in 1379 (*57*), William of Waynflete at Magdalen in 1448/58 (*59*) and Richard Fox at Corpus Christi in 1516. Each college was modelled on the one before and poached staff from it. Each of these bishops has a princely memorial chapel in Winchester Cathedral, and each has other monuments. As project manager, Wykeham built the main state-rooms at Windsor Castle for Edward III. Wayneflete built much of nearby Eton College for Henry VI. Henry Chichele, archbishop of Canterbury, founded All Souls in 1438 as a kind of war memorial for the battle of Agincourt. In 1448 that bemusing character, the creepiest of these administrator-clerics, William of Wayneflete (1395-1486), bishop of Winchester from 1447 until his death and chancellor of England in 1456-60, began to found a college by closing a road east of Logic Lane to square off the site. Having bought most of the houses there from the Hospital of St John (p.84), he realised that he could get a better site by pinching the hospital itself. He closed it down in 1458 and moved his project there, stealing all the hospital endowments, as he could while he was head of the government. In 1467 he began to rebuild the hospital as a college for 50 fellows, to designs by the master mason William Orchard, an expert in mass production, to a showy and almost gaudy design (*59 a-b*).

59a-b Above & Opposite above Magdalen College, Founder's Tower from west, the model for the Bodleian Tower (*72b*). *Photo, 1965*; detail of west doorway of chapel. *Photo, c.1935*

60a-b Opposite & Overleaf Cardinal College (now Christ Church), unfinished chapel of 1526-9: *a*) Plan of foundations discovered 1875-1964; *b*) Chapel on Agas map, north at bottom, 1578-88; note the cloister on the south side of Tom Quad, probably a short-lived timber structure put up for Queen Elizabeth's visit in 1566

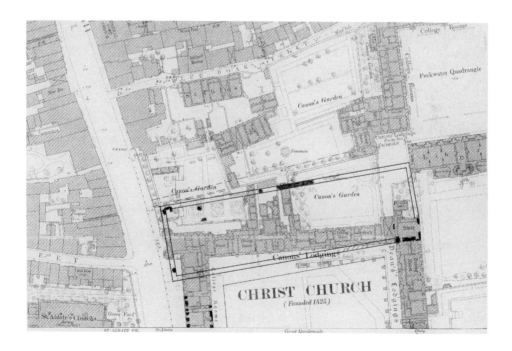

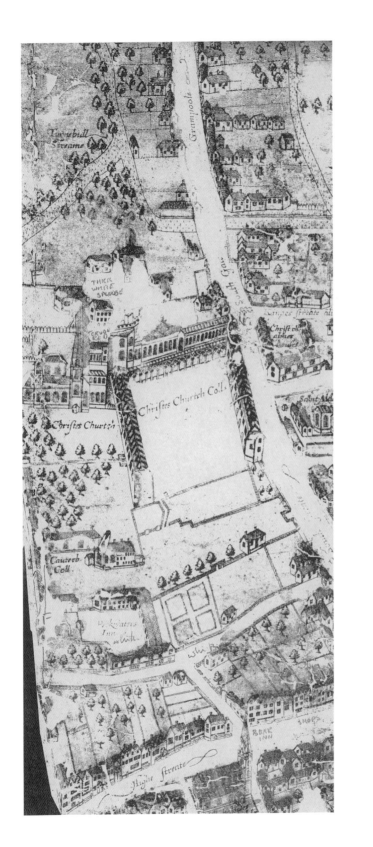

61a-e Cardinal College (now Christ Church): *a*) *Above* Detail of window-heads, left, of 1520s, right, of 1660s. *Caroe*, Wren & Tom Tower, *1923*
b) *Below* From John Bereblock's book of text and illustrations presented to Elizabeth. *Drawing, 1566*

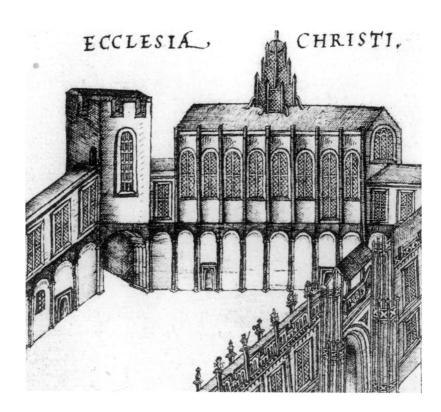

c) Above East range of Tom Quad with dean Fell and his verger. *Loggan, print, 1673;*
d) Below East range of Tom Quad with, left, north range, built by Fell and tower added by
dean Liddell. *Photo, 1965; e) Opposite* doorway inserted in south range by Alice's father,
Dean Liddell, 'HGL' in 1870. *Photo, 1975*

It was complete by 1492 when the college, eager to outdo any other, began a magnificent bell-tower (*Cover*) to outdo Merton; it was finished in 1509. A young fellow of Magdalen, Thomas Wolsey from Ipswich, supervised the construction.

In 1525 Thomas Wolsey, now the leading statesman of the day and cardinal archbishop of York, founded Cardinal College to his own glory, employing the royal master-masons Henry Redman and John Lubyns, whose magnificent, rich and sober design (*61a-e*) was two-thirds finished when Wolsey fell from power in 1529, having misjudged his monarch, Henry VIII, who arrested him and took over York Place, his London house, renaming it Whitehall Palace, and also his suburban retreat at Hampton Court, which he extended to be a great royal palace. Henry also took over and refounded Wolsey's Oxford college, leaving the chapel unfinished (p.11, *60a-b, 61a-e*). In the 1630s its walls were pulled down to be replaced by lodgings which were finally completed in the 1660s.

The tradition of bishops, worldly or politically aware, taking a hand in Oxford affairs continued for centuries and has still not entirely died away. Two college founders came to sticky ends: Walter de Merton, bishop of Rochester, caught a chill when he fell off his horse crossing a river. Walter de Stapledon, the bishop of Exeter who founded Exeter College in 1314, was an unpopular treasurer of England; when Edward II left him in charge of London, he unwisely went out for a ride. The mob caught him and two of his staff in

Cheapside, stripped them, and hacked their heads off. Two college founders were not clergymen but professional killers, who died comfortably in bed after violent lives: John de Balliol's penance for despoiling the lands of the bishop of Durham became Balliol College when his widow Devorgilla, who carried his heart round with her until she founded Sweetheart Abbey as their burial place, found that she approved of sending students to Oxford; while John Gifford, lord of many castles on the Welsh marches and victor of many fierce fights with the Welsh, founded Gloucester College.

6

ARCHITECTURE RECYCLED
& THE GHOSTS
OF LOST STRUCTURES

As well as the ghosts of people, Oxford is full of other kinds of ghosts: stumps of walls, traces of roofs, all of them signs of buildings and other structures that no longer exist, indications of lanes and streets that were closed long ago. Many of these 'other' ghosts take the form of symbols, a few words, letters or numbers, so familiar or obscure that we walk past them without taking notice. Across the city dozens of battered old stones with marks and letters, sometimes damaged, sometimes quite legible, still mark obsolete boundaries, whether of the city itself, of church parishes, of other jurisdictions, or of ownership of land. They show distances as milestones or, as bench-marks, the height above sea-level. It is not hard to find evidence that buildings have been cannibalised for re-use or recycled in quite large sections since the twelfth century or before. There have been all kinds of short-lived structures for royal visits, pageants and festivities, plays and circuses, grand balls, agricultural shows and war. In the Middle Ages, and still today, almost all large and middling building projects and most kinds of reconstructions and alterations have always required scaffolding (67), store yards fenced against petty theft, site huts and workshops (66). We glance at them every summer but somehow manage to blot them out of our consciousness, not seeing them as part of the beauty of college quadrangles and streets. There are so many of these marks and signs that we can mention only a few, starting with boundary marks of all kinds, continuing with ancient graffiti, and then going on to temporary structures and the countless signs still to be seen on historic buildings that show how they were put up, before ending with evidence for the re-use of bits or sections of older buildings in new ones.

Near the 'Ox-ford', the names Bulstake Mead and Bulstake Stream strongly suggest that, perhaps 1,000 years ago, there was a post there, carved with a bull or a bull's head or perhaps with a bull's skull nailed to it (p.8). The Local

62 City boundary stone at
78 Banbury Road, showing the Ox,
perhaps of the seventeenth century

Board District map of the 1880s shows that the city boundary was marked by three stones on the west from Hogacre Ditch to Binsey, and 18 on the north from Godstow to Parsons' Pleasure. In 1562 the City settled a dispute with the lord of the manor of Wolvercote over grazing rights by 'settynge of the mere stones in Porte meade', which suggests that some of the existing stones stand where earlier ones were put up in the sixteenth century, if not before. The section of St Clement's added to the city proper in 1832 was marked between King's Mill and the Cowley Road by six stones, all perhaps 50 years old by the 1880s. Near the foot of Magdalen Tower a badly eroded eighteenth-century milestone used to inform us that it is 54 miles from London and 8 from Woodstock. Towards the south-west corner of Radcliffe Square a large flat stone, now practically illegible, used to read 'R T', marking the corner of the block of 20 or so house-properties bought by Dr John Radcliffe's Trustees in the 1730s to form a site for the great circular library in the square that commemorates him. School Street ran north and south to the west of the stone (*20*); to the south of it a shorter unnamed street ran along the north side of St Mary's churchyard linking School Street with Cat Street. On both sides of Magpie Lane, 100m to the south on the other side of High Street, we can still see boundary stones between the parishes of St Mary the Virgin and St John the Baptist, which lost its parochial status in 1892 but remained Merton chapel. Another stone, on Henley Avenue just south of Iffley Turn (*63*), reads: 'HERE xxxxxx IFFLY HYWAY 1635'. Fifty years ago the missing word could just be made out as 'ENDETH'; it marks the southern or outer limit of one of the 'mileways' ordered by an Act of Parliament of 1576 to be maintained by residents of the villages within 5 miles of the city, but is in fact well over a mile from Magdalen Bridge. In two central streets we can still see house numbers in Roman numerals, incised to help the collectors of ground rents in the seventeenth century, long before street numbers were introduced. Merton owned almost the whole of Holywell and introduced house numbers in 1663, so that No.3 is marked III, No.26 is XVIII, and the former No.54, opposite the Music Room, is XXXII. Brasenose owned the site of St Mary's College in New Inn Hall Street, where the present Nos 22 and 24 are numbered XIII on a replaced door-lintel and XIV on an old one. These marker stones or numbers are never entirely permanent and tend to disappear in casual alterations, repaving or refacing. A triangle of York stone paving in High Street just to the west of Queen's Lane was marked 'QC', to show that Queen's College really owned that patch of land, given up when the front of the college was built in the eighteenth century; the mark disappeared in the 1970s when the pavement was relaid. In Brasenose College a stone shield at the south end of the passage leading south from the Front Quad was dated '16/09', crucial evidence for the creation of the passage and, most probably, for most of the windows in the Front Quad. In the early 1990s the stone was replaced with a blank undated shield; the bursar, quizzed about the date-stone which he had walked past thousands of times, replied that he was 'not aware of its existence'.

Many inscriptions or plaques have been put up to commemorate historical events and eminent characters, self-conscious ghosts cut in stone. By the Botanic Garden gate, just across the road from Magdalen tower, a bilingual plaque records that the Jews' burial ground was here (p.85-6). The dramatic events of 1555, when an archbishop and two bishops were burnt at the stake

63 Mileways stone of 1635 on Henley Avenue near Iffley Turn. *Photo, c.1970*

on the edge of the Town Ditch in Broad Street, are commemorated by a wealth of structures, plaques, mementoes and records. Among them are the Martyrs' Memorial at the south end of St Giles, built by G.G. Scott in 1841–3 for an ad-hoc low-church committee; the chancel and north aisle of St Mary Magdalen, rebuilt by Scott in 1841 with the committee's surplus funds; a plaque on Balliol College; the stone cross flush with the surface of Broad Street succeeding a stone of 1749; the reputed prison door at St Michael's; a burnt stump stored away in the Ashmolean basement; and any number of reported finds of ash up and down Broad Street. And yet the martyrs were all Cambridge men without any Oxford connections, apart from their tragic end. In Gloucester Green we read that the ringleaders of a group of mutinous Roundhead soldiers were shot, no doubt deservedly, somewhere in that area. The great scientist Robert Boyle is mentioned on a stone in front of the Shelley Memorial at University College which tells us: 'Here he discovered Boyle's Law and made experiments with an AIR PUMP designed by his assistant ROBERT HOOKE, Inventor, Scientist & Architect…'. A historian of science once trapped me there and explained at length that every part of this inscription was, strictly speaking, untrue. These inscriptions tend to come and go, like date-stones and ownership marks. Even king Richard I, 'the Lionheart', born in Oxford in 1157, disappeared a few years ago from Beaumont Street when a stone column, perhaps not far from the site of the royal palace (p.43), was knocked down by chance or vandals, but has just been replaced. In the next street a plaque on 12 St John Street used to record that Mensa, the elitist high-IQ society, was founded there in 1946; this claim was untrue and the plaque was removed in the 1990s.

It is always worth admiring the great oak tables in college dining halls, whose legs are often great doric columns. Some of those at Christ Church date from 1598/9; a group at University College may date from c.1610–30, before the present hall was completed in 1656. Brasenose had a set of new tables made in 1683/4. We should also examine them closely top and bottom for names, initials, sketches (an elegant regency yacht at Christ Church seems to have been sanded away in the 1990s) and game boards, such as can be found underneath an ancient table at Jesus, which at some time must have been turned over. These tables are regularly moved out to make room for dances and concerts and have, underneath, a variety of chalk marks and numbered paper labels to help the college staff put them back in the right place. The fifteenth-century choir stalls of St Mary the Virgin provide a rich haul of Elizabethan and Jacobean names, as well as a game board for use behind gowned arms during lengthy sermons or academic meetings. Tourists too have scratched their names and the date on medieval monuments in the Cathedral since the 1620s and (with more energy and better tools), into the stonework of the viewing platform round the base of St Mary's spire.

Most of medieval Oxford has disappeared; many of the churches (p.45) have been demolished, rebuilt or transferred to new sites. Almost all the medieval houses have been rebuilt or taken down and most of their sites are quite unrecognisable. There were some 700 house properties within the walled town and another 500 in the suburbs. In the north-east corner of the town, New College and its magnificent gardens occupy 35 or more former house- properties and several lanes, while in the south-east corner Merton and its splendid garden take up another 15 or so medieval properties and the site of the parish church of St John (pp.106-8). Fully a tenth of the walled town lies beneath Christ Church, including 60 or so house properties, the synagogue (p.11, 45, 2), a parish church, the first home of the Blackfriars (p.61), the Priory of St Frideswide (pp.55-8, 22a-b, 23a-b), three streets and a 250m length of the Town Wall itself. This part of medieval Oxford is not easy to reconstruct on paper, even with the help of hundreds of medieval deeds and key surviving structures. The two east–west streets can be confidently located by surviving garden walls, in one case confirmed by excavation (*colour plate 5*), and the priory church survives, almost complete, as Oxford Cathedral, with three of its four cloister ranges. The failure of archaeologists in the late 1960s to cover two building schemes in the college has left two large gaps, unfortunately permanent, in our knowledge of medieval Oxford (*11*). Watching briefs there would have helped to indentify and locate two groups of medieval house properties.

If we change our focus from college sites to details of stonework, we can easily pick out on the chapels of New College and Merton the positions and sizes of massive squared timbers used for scaffolding when they were built. At New College, in a passage beneath the dining hall, we can also see two wide archways left by the stonemasons so that the principal roof timbers could be carted into place and hoisted up, after which the arches were blocked. Many of the city's buildings contain parts and signs of older buildings that were being dismantled when the newer ones that we see were put up. At Carfax, on the tower of St Martin's church at the very centre of the modern city, we can see where the church stood until 1896 from a steeply-pitched roofline (*colour plate 13b*). This is in fact just one, probably the earliest, of three rooflines that were exposed, as we see from a drawing made in 1897 (*81b*). The higher of the two low-pitched rooflines marks the roof of the church rebuilt in 1820-2 (*81a*); the lower of them marks the raising of the walls in *c*.1400 to light the nave with clerestory windows (*26d*), while the steep-pitched roofline, the one we see today, may be earlier still, of the twelfth or thirteenth century.

The Town Wall is easy to follow; we can walk outside or inside it, sometimes both, as it runs around the heart of the town (p.79). A fine stretch of this not very defensive wall survives in New College garden over 400m, with six surviving wall-towers or bastions (p.81), but we can follow the whole course for 2030m inside or outside, and sometimes both. It needs imagination to visualise low rubble walls as being as splendid as the length in New College. Most stretches of the Wall have a history well recorded in the city archives, which allows us to grasp how each stretch reached its present form. We may note one

64 Mason's mark in cloister of St Frideswide's Priory (Christ Church), fifteenth century. *Photo, c.1990*

example, where Brewer Street runs into St Aldate's. Early in 1617 the City Council ordered the South Gate to be taken down as it was collapsing. Demolition cost five shillings (25p). More stone for a proposed rebuilding was delivered for 16 shillings (80p). It was left stacked on site just beside the grandiose Tudor architecture of Christ Church, but the gate was never rebuilt. Some of the 'City stones lying before Christ Church' was used in 1619 to mend a lock in the river at Fisher Row. The rest was left piled up in the street for another seven years until, in 1623, the City gave them all to a prosperous local bookseller and binder, George Chambers, to build a large house on city land beside the castle.

One group of building craftsmen, carpenters, possessed the skills required for temporary buildings and scaffolds; they could also put up smaller structures, like houses or roofs, without much or any scaffolding. Almost all their work was prefabricated, made in the yard or on site before being hoisted into position and pegged together. Practically every roof and every timber building could be taken apart, and often still can be, allowing the individual timbers to be moved, mended or replaced. In 1605, when James I paid a ceremonial visit to Oxford, two remarkable theatres were set up, a new classical playhouse in the dining hall at Christ Church and a refurbished old theatre for graduation ceremonies at St Mary's church (*65*). Both are well documented with plans and can be precisely related to the spaces for which they were designed. The 'theatre' at St Mary's was first set up in 1565 by two master carpenters, Richard Brimpton and William Peckover, each of whom had a small family business employing perhaps two to four journeymen with much the same number of apprentices. By the terms of university's contract with them, Brimpton and Peckover had to give up their 'freedom' of the city and become 'privileged' members of the university. Every summer, on ten days' notice, they had to take the 'frame' out of its store in the old congregation house (*44b*), replace any

damaged or broken timbers, and set it up round St Mary's nave with all the
necessary seats, desks and benches from the same store, adapting them for any
special requirements. After the Vespers and the Act had been celebrated they
had to put the whole thing away again. This went on for a century, until the
temporary 'theatre' was replaced in 1669 by the Sheldonian Theatre, designed
by our astronomy professor Christopher Wren for the same academic ceremonies. The Oxford theatre of 1565 may have influenced the London carpenter James Burbage when, 11 years later in 1576, having turned to acting,
he built the Theatre at Shoreditch; it was polygonal, not rectangular, but it
could also be taken down and put up again, as Burbage's sons famously did after
a dispute with their landlord in 1599. With other actors and playwrights, among
them Shakespeare, they dismantled the Theatre and reassembled it on Bankside
as the Globe, no doubt having to adapt and replace some of the timbers.
Oxford's 'theatre' had quite an impact on local carpenters. One of Peckover's

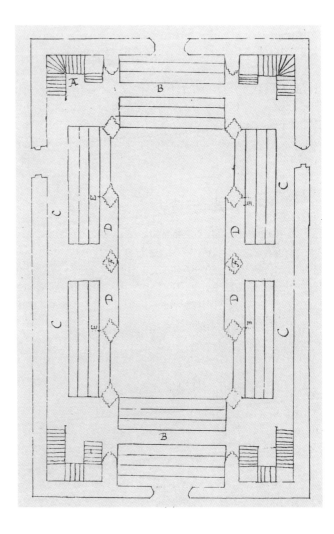

65 The 'theatre' at St
Mary's church, 1605

66 Masons' lodge at Magdalen Hall (Hertford College) in 1820. *Mackenzie and Skelton, print, 1825*

67 Scaffolding at Magdalen Hall (Hertford College) in 1820. *Mackenzie and Skelton, print, 1825*

sons followed him as a master carpenter while two other sons went up to Christ Church and took their degrees. One was ordained, became a country parson, then an archdeacon and ended up as canon of Salisbury. Thanks to the university's insistence on its own particular pair of carpenters taking 'privilege', they joined the other master craftsmen under academic control, such as book-sellers, bookbinders, stationers, parchment-sellers, cooks, apothecaries, bar-bers, surgeons and carriers; the university also licensed or supervised vintners, tavern-keepers, brewers, brownbakers and whitebakers, and tried to extend its sway over leather-sellers and other trades.

When promoters of change are not quite sure how their project will turn out, they sometimes put up 'mock-ups' to see how it will look and find out what people will say about it. In the mid-1960s St Edmund Hall put up a row of plywood gables to persuade the city planners that the east range of the new upper quad would not be visible from Magdalen Bridge. It was all too visible, but the scheme was allowed and the concrete gables of 1969 are permanently visible. At much the same time Carfax Conduit (70), an elaborately carved stone watertank of 1616, suddenly appeared in the middle of Broad Street in the course of an elaborate debate about whether to liven the street up by mov-ing the Martyrs' Memorial there or something. This fake conduit looked somehow unconvincing, as it was made of wood and canvas, with the carving painted on; the real one, at grass in Nuneham Park since the city gave it to Harcourt in 1787, is happily still there. In the early 1870s Henry Liddell, dean of Christ Church and father of *Alice in Wonderland,* and his current architect George Gilbert Scott enjoyed themselves enormously, pulling the college around and transforming Tom Quad (*68a*). Wondering whether to raise the nave roof to the steep pitch visible, as a 'fossil' on the tower they mocked up a gable which showed how much a high roof would dominate the quad. Scott claimed that the Cathedral tower was cracking, so they moved the bells into a big wooden box built over the hall stairs in 1872. This enraged the fictional Alice's creator, C.L. Dodgson, who spent months on a pamphlet war, dubbing it the 'meat-safe'. In 1876-8 this crude wooden bell-box was screened by a handsome low tower designed by Thomas Garner, whose partnership won a competition against Scott. By then the college was £90,000 in debt and an ornate timber superstructure that Garner had designed had to be left off, and the temporary wooden belfry was simply left standing within the tower walls. When the stone cresting and openwork battlements needed repair and were dismantled in 1975, the 'meat-safe' popped up again into view (*68b*), and remained visible for many months while a furious debate raged in governing body about whether a modern architect could out-Garner Garner. The tower now again looks as it did in 1878; its over-emphatic corner pinnacles still lack their whole reason for existing, the fancy timber topping; and the bells still ring out from the temporary 'meat-safe' of 1872.

68 Tom Quad, Christ Church, south-east corner: *a)* *Above* Temporary wooden belfry in centre, with wooden mock-ups of, left; steep-pitched nave roof, right; openwork parapet on hall roof and, far right; battlements on Staircase 1. *Photo, 1872*; *b)* *Opposite* Belfry showing above dismantled cresting of tower, 1975

In 1928 another college, Magdalen, suffered from growing pains and evicted my old school from its handsome schoolroom of 1849-51 (now the college library), designed by J.C. Buckler, the artist and antiquarian, and from the playground behind, where the school once beat the university at hockey by 16 goals to one, playing the school's own lethal game with ash sticks and a hard ball which could be bounced off the buttresses and kept in play. On the old school site the college itself built handsome stone Gothic ranges to Sir Giles Scott's design in 1928-30. The school, in Cowley Place across Magdalen Bridge, was not so lucky. Its temporary building of 1928 was a flimsy timber-framed job held together with wire mesh and clad in roughcast. After I went there in 1945, I baked in summer and shivered in winter, most of all in the fearsome winter of blizzards and fuel shortages in '47 when we sat for week after week in uninsulated, unheated classrooms, only our Latin master bringing a bit of cheer into our lives with the oil stove that he carried everywhere with him. At least all germs were frozen too, as all the classroom doors opened on to fresh air; and we suffered from no epidemics until 1954, my last year, when a new three-storey classroom block brought raging influenza and the school had to close for several days. But some of the 1920s building is still in daily use.

On Port Meadow we can find short-lived military remains of two quite different periods: at the south end a length of Sir Thomas Fairfax's siegeworks of the summer of 1646 (*3*), and at the north an aerodrome used in 1912-18.

Most of this area contains faint marks of tents and tracks and, as the planes took off and landed on grass, there are no obvious runways. But there are two substantial monuments above ground level, the first a memorial plaque to the two airmen killed in 1912 in an early fatal air crash, the second a concrete bunker set in the damp ditch on the Meadow that marks the old Wolvercote parish boundary. Built, so local rumour asserts, in *c*.1916 for strafing practice, it is still handy for sheltering in from heavy showers unless the cows get there first. From the same war 'differences of texture in the lawn at the far end of the garden' at New College 'marked the sites where there had been hospital tents for wounded soldiers' until the 1930s. During the Second World War, the streets of Oxford and our school playground, as I can well recall, housed a number of shoddy smelly brick air-raid shelters, real deathtraps with flat concrete roofs. Many college quadrangles contained 'static water tanks' of sheet steel, some-times reinforced with brickwork or earth, not unlike a defensive rampart.

69a-e Opposite & Above Some lost Oxford buildings: *a*) *Top left* A carved doorway of 1525-6 at Cardinal College, destroyed 1975; *b*) *Top right* Part of alderman Wright's Jacobean house on the Town Wall, taken down and installed on the Turl by G.G. Scott in 1856, demolished 1962; *c*) *Bottom left* The old Clarendon Hotel, in fact the Tudor Star Inn, demolished 1954; *d*) *Bottom right* Exeter College, west range of North Quad, built by G.G. Scott in 1858, demolished 1962; *e*) *Above* The Curator's House at the University Museum, demolished 1955

Around the edge of the city, to halt tank attacks, there were concrete pyramids and movable barriers, pathetic and moving defences of those defiant days. The broken-up fragments, tipped onto waste ground or into the Oxford Canal, can still cause problems and puncture rubber dinghies. Just after the war, in 1946, New College paid the skilled local builders, Knowles & Son, £1946 to defile their lawns over the medieval Town Ditch with three long ranges of squat 'Orlit' pre-cast concrete huts, the most hideous structures ever put up by any college, had they been permanent. To help erect them Knowles's acquired all kinds of useful equipment, such as concrete mixers, a small petrol crane (£355) and tubular steel scaffolding (£755), which that rather old-fashioned firm had never previously needed, as well as a regular fleet of lorries, trucks, vans and cars.

Every church and every college in the city must have contained recycled building material. In the 1190s the canons of St Frideswide's launched a building appeal, pleading that their church had been burnt down. They may have been referring only to the roofs of a church of *c*.1100, and then only to the south transept and nave; the rest of the priory church seems to have been rebuilt with stone vaults in *c*.1160-80. In the south transept close examination shows that there are old carved stones re-used in inconspicuous high places, while in several places at ground level burnt stones, turned through a right angle and re-cut, can be spotted where a line of pinkish red shows up against the creamy-white limestone. In the 1650s Brasenose got a chapel roof of the 1520s, which had come from the former St Mary's College, later Frewin Hall. In the 1710s the foundations of the old Whitefriars, on the site of Beaumont Street, were grubbed up for rubble for the deep footings of the Clarendon Building (78).

7

ANTHONY WOOD'S *HISTORY:*
BOOKS & LIBRARIES
IN STUART OXFORD

In 1668 Dr John Fell (1625-86), the sublimely arrogant dean of Christ Church, largest and richest of the colleges, established the university press. He was dean (*61c*) from 1660 to 1686 and also bishop of Oxford from 1675. No one had the courage to suggest that it was bad form, if not uncanonical, to hold both senior posts in the same Cathedral. The press, ostensibly an academic business, was in fact a partnership with Thomas Yate, principal of Brasenose, Sir Leoline Jenkins (1623-85), principal of Jesus, and Sir Joseph Williamson (1633-1701). Before Fell's time the university had allowed some local printers, like Joseph Barnes, to describe themselves as 'printer to the university'. Fell and his partners published 150 books, most of them in Greek, Arabic, Hebrew, Syriac and Welsh; his scheme for a Malay gospel failed. Four of his books, published in 1674-7, have a special Oxford interest. Fell himself paid the production costs of Anthony Wood's *Historia et Antiquitates Universitatis Oxoniensis* (1674, 2 vols) and, in his high-handed way, insisted on having it translated into Latin; he felt that he should be able to alter and rewrite it as he chose. David Loggan's *Oxonia Illustrata* (1675), with 40 plates showing the main university and college buildings (*18b, 26b, 52, 56a, 61c, 71, 72a*), was intended to be an illustrated supplement to Wood's history. These two books transformed for ever the way we think of Oxford and the way we see it. Humphrey Prideaux's *Marmora Oxoniensia* (1676) introduced to the learned world some special antiquities, Oxford's Greek and Roman inscriptions. Robert Plot's *Natural History of Oxfordshire* (1677) gives a readable general survey of the county, in English rather than Latin. Fell's residence, the Deanery at Christ Church, still stands (*61c*), as do the Oxford homes of both Wood and Loggan. Robert Plot's old family home in Kent also survives, allowing us to feel close to them all. David Loggan (1634-92) was born in Danzig (now Gdansk), the son of a local widow and an Anglo-Scottish immigrant, perhaps a commercial agent. The city, nominally Polish, was dominated by rich German

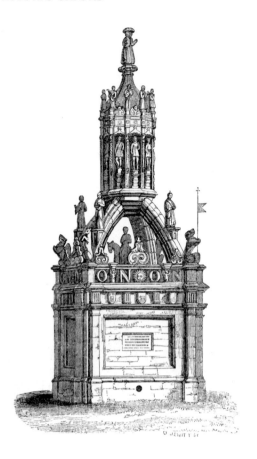

70 Carfax Conduit, built in 1616 by John Clark, a Yorkshire stonemason, and paid for by a London lawyer, Otho Nicholson. This watertank, richly carved and gilt, supplied fresh water to the city until 1787; it stood in the centre of the main crossroads

merchants, set in a county of 30 villages, overwhelmingly German until the 1940s. Willem Hondius who flourished in Danzig in *c.*1636-52, may have trained him as an artist and engraver and sent him through a network of relatives and fellow-engravers to Amsterdam to work for Crispijn de Passe the younger. By 1656 Loggan was established as a portrait-artist and engraver in London; by 1665 he was working in Oxford. He already had relatives in Oxfordshire, as his great-grandfather Robert Loggan had migrated south from Scotland in *c.*1570 to become a prosperous yeoman farmer and petty squire at Little Tew and Idbury. Robert's fifth son Edward (d. 1636) moved 20 miles away to Bretforton, near Evesham in Worcestershire, and his son John (b. 1608), the most adventurous of them all, moved over 800 miles east to the Baltic coast of Poland. Humphrey Prideaux (1648-1724) was born in 1648 and educated at Westminster School and Christ Church, where dean Fell took him up. Robert Plot (1641-96) was the son of a minor country gentleman of Sutton Baron at Borden, near Sittingbourne in Kent, and studied at Magdalen Hall. His father, a militia captain, is commemorated by a warlike monument with trophies of arms and cannon.

Anthony Wood (1632-95), greatest of all historians of Oxford, was born in Postmasters Hall (*46*) in Merton Street where he lived for almost all his life. In 1647-52, in the uneasy days of the Commonwealth, he studied just across the road at Merton College (*52*). After taking his degree he devoted his life to local history, without having to find an academic post or go into trade, as a small private income let him go through life doing exactly what he wanted to. His family had moved south from Lancashire in the 1560s; his father's fortune seems to have come from inns in London and Islington owned by his grandfather's godfather, Robert Wood, and from prudent marriages. His grandfather Richard Wood of Islington (*c.*1536-94) married Elizabeth Jackson (d. 1596) daughter of an Oxford draper, whose son was a fellow of Corpus Christi College. When she died the draper, Henry Jackson senior, became guardian to Wood's father Thomas (1581-1643) and his teenage siblings, each due to inherit £500. In 1603 Thomas took his BA from Corpus, married Margaret Wood (d. 1621), 'an ancient and rich maid' with a dowry, and took up farming at

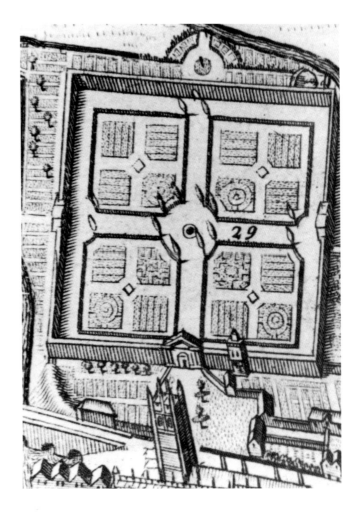

71 The Physic (now Botanic) Garden, with wall and gates (*cover, 82*) built by the London mason Nicholas Stone, and planted in the 1630s, bird's-eye view from north. *Loggan, print, 1675*

143

Tetsworth west of Oxford. In 1608 he bought Postmasters Hall on a Merton College lease and, in 1616, Fleur-de-Lys, an inn just south of Carfax also on a Merton lease. He also may have traded in wine and run the inn in a rather hands-off way, as he took a minor law degree and perhaps practised as a lawyer. He had an apprentice, another Thomas Wood, later his servant. In 1622 the first Thomas Wood married Mary Pettie of Wyfold, a much younger woman with a good dowry, who gave him six sons, five of whom survived to adulthood. Anthony, the fourth, lost his father when he was ten years old and never managed to find out much about him. The family home, Postmasters Hall (46), once part of Merton and then an academic hall, still stands, and Wood's books, diaries and notes of monthly expenses give us unrivalled insights into his daily life, his neighbours in St John's parish, and the whole social make-up of Restoration Oxford and its region.

He bequeathed his research papers and books, with his vast collections of plays, ballads, leaflets, chapbooks, newspapers, pamphlets and almanacs, to the Ashmolean Museum; and the Bodleian Library now has practically all of them in its care. Wood's executor, Arthur Charlett, master of University College, was not as meticulous as he could have been, and for some years after his death, Wood's papers kept turning up among his papers; several interesting batches of them are still among the archives of University College. Wood's family must be one of the best recorded 'middle-class' families of the seventeenth century. He left us with many mysteries, although he is by far the most completely documented scholar of the time. Thanks to his habit of jotting down notes about any matters which came to his attention, his home parish of St John the Baptist, Oxford, is among the most minutely attested corner of any English town in Stuart times. Most of the parishioners earned their living by hospitality and entertainment; and Wood's family income, which allows us to think of him as a dedicated 'gentleman scholar', came from the Merton Street tennis court and its alehouse, in which players quenched their thirst, and from the Fleur-de-Lys inn just south of Carfax, all leased from Merton. Except for the Woods, who lived at Postmasters Hall for a century or more, and held the lease from 1608 until the 1740s, the other families all came and went, staying for a few decades or just a few years. St John's parish was small, only 3.5ha, packed with academic institutions, the whole of Merton College with its extensive gardens, St Alban Hall, with the south-east corner of Oriel College and the east part of Corpus Christi College. Only St Martin's, of 2ha, and All Saints, of 2.8ha, both in the very centre of the city and full of prosperous citizens' houses, were smaller. In the 1660s there were three large old houses on Merton Street (46), one of which, in multiple occupation, was subdivided into five or six dwellings, and was known as 'The Pit'. There were two more houses on the east–west lane to the north and three more further north still on Magpie Lane, so that in the 1660s 14 families lived in the parish. In 1680 the west wing of 'The Pit' was reconstructed as four cottages and the Window Tax of 1696 lists 16 families.

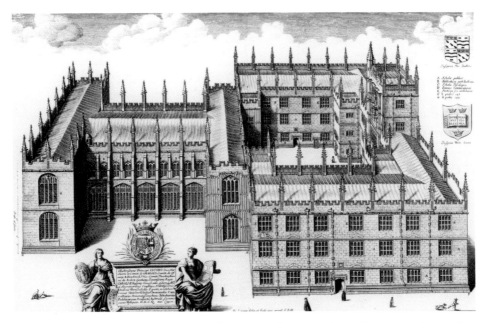

72a-b Bodleian Library tower and Schools Quadrangle, 1613-18. *a) Above* From the south. *Loggan, Print, 1675 b) Below* From the east, 1820. *Mackenzie & Skelton, print, 1820*; the master carpenter Thomas Holt (*74*) installed the floors and roof

The most feckless, the local problem family, consisted of Richard Barefoot, letter carrier, 'and his ragged crew' (as Wood described them in 1662) in the east wing of 'The Pit'. They lived there for at least 65 years, longer than most families. Richard's son Edmund died in 1647 and his granddaughter Eleanor or 'Ketcher' Repingale, 'receiver of alms', in 1722. In between, his granddaughters Anne and Sarah Repinghale died in 1668 and 1672; he died in 1674, his married daughter, Alice or 'Brass' Repingale in 1682, his widow Ann, 'receiver of alms', in 1700 and his son-in-law John or 'Catcher' Rippingale, 'receiver of alms' in 1706. Whatever the parish may have thought of them as a burden on their generosity, most other Barefoots and Rippingales were respectable farmers in north-west Oxfordshire. There were a few tailors. Richard Hearne from Binsey, who counted Anthony Wood among his customers in the 1660s, had a room or two in 'The Pit', and was succeeded there by another tailor, Jeffrey Clerk, who made Wood a 'new studying gowne' in 1678. The rest of the parishioners were almost all college cooks and under-cooks, butlers and under-butlers in short-lived dynasties, coming from outside Oxford, son succeeding father, and then going away again after two or three generations. Nathaniel Jeans, head butler of Merton who died in 1661, owned houses elsewhere in the city (75) and had another business, an alehouse and cookshop that he and his wife ran in their nearby house in the large and populous parish of St Peter in the East. After his death his widow Katherine continued the cookshop; its foundations lie under the north-east corner of the Examination Schools Quadrangle. From 1657 to 1670 Wood often ate there and spent many congenial evenings with friends, calling it Jeanes', mother Jeanes' or 'a certaine club'. Nathaniel's brother Daniel Jeanes was butler of St Alban Hall, while his son Thomas, who died in 1687, succeeded him as head butler of Merton and lived just across the road from the college chapel in the south-west corner of 'The Pit'. The other specialist occupation in that part of Oxford was medicine; the celebrated Dr Thomas Willis (1621-75) lived at Beam Hall (46), before moving to London in 1666.

Just across High Street, Radcliffe Square (in Wood's day Cat Street and School Street) is mostly composed of libraries, a striking and varied architectural ensemble of c.1450-1750. The area, dominated by magnificent containers for books, now lacks bookshops, but we have noted (pp.93,99) that as long ago as the thirteenth century this was the heart of the Oxford book world, long before any of the libraries were built. Ever since then, this part of Oxford has been dominated by books, which have always been able to force mere people out of their way. One family driven out by the relentless pressure of books and the need for teaching space was called Cheynell, living in a house in Cat Street which they leased from Magdalen College. John Cheynell, head of the family, had come from Surrey to Corpus Christi College as a scholar in 1581, took his degree in 1583 and later qualified in medicine. By his first wife, Rebecca, who died in 1605, he had four children, John, Margaret, Leonard and Johanna; the two boys survived their father but the two girls died in childhood. By a second wife, Bridget, he had another four children, Francis (1608-65), Martha, Bridget and Alice. In 1613 they had to leave Cat Street and move to Holywell, to make room for the Schools Quadrangle, now Old Bodleian Library (*72b*), on which work began that year. John Cheynell died that year, leaving a will, now in the university archives, in which he left the eldest son John £20 a year and his great silver-gilt salt 'with the pelican on the toppe', the great silver goblet, a dozen silver spoons and a great brass pot, while Leonard was to get £140 and a broad silver-gilt bowl and a little silver bowl. Martha was to have £100 when she came of age; Bridget and Alice were to get similar portions, and Francis, then five years old, was left the lease of Rewley Mead, on the Botley Road, which his father held from Corpus, his old college. Cheynell's widow found a new husband, the bishop of Salisbury, Robert Abbot (1560-1617), whose younger brother George (1562-1633) was archbishop of Canterbury. Francis went up to Merton, where his stepfather's kinsman, Nathaniel Brent (1573-1652) was warden, and was elected a fellow in 1629, leading on to a career as a celebrated and resolute presbyterian, army chaplain, professor of divinity and president of St John's College, only to be ejected from all his posts in 1660. In 1941, during the Second World War, the authorities of the Bodleian Library installed an underground watertank just where the Cheynells' backyard had been before their house was demolished in 1613. In 1958, when I went to work at the Ashmolean Museum, I found several boxes of unwashed potsherds found when the watertank was dug out, together with a few larger bits of pot that had been washed and catalogued. With volunteers from local schools I scrubbed the pottery, stuck together the sherds that fitted together and drew and published the pots that were more or less complete (*73a*). They must represent the family's breakages over the last few years before they left, thrown into a stone-lined cesspit which was never cleaned out after the university took over the site in 1613. Dr Cheynell's will detailing his plate does not mention pots.

Hundreds of St Mary's parishioners, the medieval scribes, illuminators, parchment-makers and bookbinders, lie buried in the churchyard beside the square, together with hundreds more from the age of printing: bookbinders, perhaps the oldest of the existing trades in that world, typefounders, printers, stationers, and booksellers. The booksellers, driven out by libraries and their piles of books, have taken refuge in nearby streets, while the other trades have had to move away. School Street, parallel to Cat Street, can be recognised in outline on the west side of Radcliffe Square (*20*). This street still has one surviving house, if only its back wing, in the narrow part of the street now called St Mary's Entry, just to the west of St Mary's church. We can see a porch, largely a late Victorian fantasy, with, on the old timber doorposts, a coat of arms with a diagonal chequerboard. This fairly large wing of a house was incorporated into Brasenose College more than a century ago, but we can see from the porch, and from the way the house was timber-framed with overhanging upper

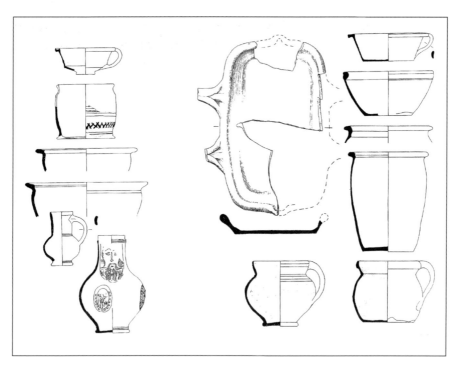

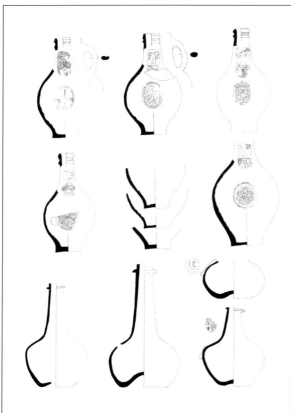

73a-b a) *Above* Pottery broken by the Cheynell family, *c.*1610–13; their house in Cat Street stood to the south or left of the Bodleian tower (pp.146–7, *72b*); b) *Left* Richard Smith's cookhouse in Broad Street; glass bottles for serving wine and cider, and stoneware bottles for drinking beer floors, that it really was a house. The coat of arms tells us, as we learn to read that special language, that it once belonged to Magdalen College. Among the deeds and leases at Magdalen, put into print by H.E. Salter, it takes only a few minutes to work out that this was the home and business premises of Joseph Barnes (d. 1620), printer to the university. As well as printing books and pamphlets, he sold books, published books and, holding a license for a wine-tavern, also sold wine as an extra source of income, just in case Oxford people ever stopped reading. If we stand at the porch and turn to face the church, we should be able to see, on the stonework of the church between the buttresses of the north and south aisles, traces of two narrow lock-up bookshops on either side of the west door of the church. But much of the stonework here seems to have been refaced, leaving no patches of new stone where beams had been set into the walls. The whole of this part of Oxford is full of bookshops, remains of bookshops and ghosts of bookshops, and also of images of books. One of the corbels holding up the roof of the oldest part of the Bodleian Library shows a winged angel holding out a book, in a kind of heavenly book-delivery service. Several nearby college chapels have monuments formed with books, also carved in stone. At Wadham Thomas Harris, son of a mayor of Oxford, was commemorated in the brand-new college chapel by a modest tablet framed with books when he died tragically young in 1614, after a few months as one of the founding fellows. Sir Thomas Bodley's splendid monument at Merton has piles of books standing in for classical columns, in a mannerist conceit (53). In the same chapel Bodley's friend, Sir Henry Savile, warden of the college 1585-1622, has a matching monument with figures of Dio Chrysostom and Ptolemy on one side and of Euclid and Tacitus on the other, which refer to his published editions of their works. Savile played a major part in devising and introducing the characteristic Oxford bookcase of the late sixteenth and seventeenth centuries, splendid structures of oak, themselves well worth close archaeological scrutiny.

In an area so steeped in books and libraries, the archaeology of libraries and of bookcases has a special fascination. Radcliffe Square and the area round has plenty of recorded archaeology, as the impact of books by the tens of thousand, of storing them and keeping them safe from fire, has led to all kinds of building projects and to many archaeological observations and discoveries, above and below ground, over the last 100 years. At Merton we can see, in the west wing of the library, the two-shelf bookcases designed by Sir Henry Savile (1549-1622) and made by the joiner Thomas Key and, in the south wing, another run of bookcases made in 1623, just after Savile's death, by William Bennet, a leading Oxford joiner. At the Bodleian we can admire the tall three-shelf bookcases made in 1599-1600 for Sir Thomas Bodley by Key and Bennet in partnership. Unusually for a master craftsman of his time, Bennet seems to have been illiterate, as he made a mark instead of signing his name. He was quite a fiery character, as he accidentally killed a college cook in 1590 in some affray. Despite this, academic patrons demanding the best generally chose him above the 12 or so other master joiners

74a-b Thomas Holt, a Yorkshire carpenter working in Oxford, and his men loved carving fleur-de-lys on doorposts: *a) Left* His own house at No.17 Holywell. *Photo, 2004: b) Right* The buttery doorway at Oriel, *c*.1639, found and plastered over again. *Photo, 1971*

in the town, except in Arts End, the west wing added to Duke Humfrey in 1611-12. Thomas Bolton, more a carver than a joiner, seems to have installed the novel wall-shelves and galleries there; Bodley wrote to his librarian 'I am sorie for Benet, whose skill I shall want in many respects; but yet my trust is in Bolten'. At the other end of Duke Humfrey, the east wing, long known as 'Selden End' has bold columned galleries and wall-shelving made in 1639-41 by Bennet's son-in-law Thomas Richardson, who took over his business and assets. Richardson, with more than the rudiments of education and book-learning, wrote out the specification and signed it in his bold Italic hand. His uncle was Joseph Barnes, the university printer (p.141); and in 1643, a few years later, his younger cousin, Mary Powell of Forest Hill, married the poet John Milton. Her father Richard could pose as a petty country squire, but was really a hard-working timber dealer who often appears in college accounts selling trees from Stowood and elsewhere for the many building projects of the time.

Between 1608 and 1642 local masons and carpenters, with many newcomers, enjoyed one of Oxford's greatest building booms, as the city's non-academic

75 No.23 Pembroke Street, a property of Nathaniel Jeans, head butler of Merton College, with a projecting top-floor window; the street was burnt down in the great fire of 1644, but soon rebuilt. It is not a pair with No.24, (right), a Christ Church house leased to Joseph Williams, carpenter of St Ebbe's. Note the scaffold on No.20 (left), based in barrels of earth. The houses are now part of Pembroke College. *Taunt, photo, c.1900*

population grew rapidly and students flooded into the colleges and halls. Patrons, well-wishers and old members gave generously towards building projects to house vastly increased numbers. The university itself built a large quadrangle of lecture rooms, the Schools Quadrangle of 1613-18 (*72a-b*), for which much of the funding came from London livery companies. At Merton, the warden, Sir Henry Savile, younger son of a prosperous landowning family in Yorkshire, built the large Fellows Quadrangle in 1608-10 (*52*), bringing masons and carpenters from around Halifax in his native county, so much did he mistrust Oxford builders. Dorothy Wadham, elderly widow of a rich old-fashioned squire with estates in Devon and Somerset, built a large new college, Wadham, in 1610-13, with the help of stonemasons from Stoke-sub-Hamdon, one of the quarry villages beside Ham Hill in Somerset. As well as distrusting Oxford builders she also, at first, distrusted any farmers and carters that her steward might hire to bring down stone from the quarries at Headington into Oxford. She went so far as to send her own waggons and ox-teams from Merifield, near Ilminster in Somerset, on the gruelling six-day trek to Oxford, but only for the first building season in

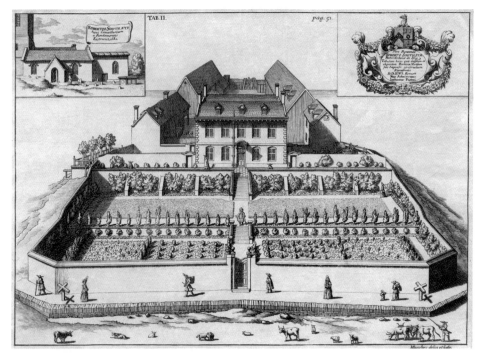

76 Islip Rectory, 8km north of Oxford, was built in 1692 for Robert South (1634-1716), canon of Westminster and Christ Church, noted for amusing and pithy sermons, even at court. In 1713 he refused the bishopric of Rochester, unlike Walter de Merton in the thirteenth century. *M. Burghers, print, 1695*

1610. Other colleges kept pace as fast as they could afford to or find the builders, who added and rebuilt as colleges or their patrons requested, at Brasenose, Exeter, Jesus, Lincoln, Oriel, Pembroke, St John's and University College. Several colleges rebuilt or refitted their old libraries during rebuilding projects of this time, scrapping the medieval bookcases. At Jesus a brand-new library, built on pillars in 1626, started to crack and had to be dismantled in 1637; the college got a local joiner to make a careful drawing when he took the bookcases out. After 40 years in storage, while the books endured various makeshift arrangements, the bookcases found a new home by about 1679 in a splendid new library. At Christ Church we can see a medieval building, the old dining hall of St Frideswide's Priory, used as a college library from *c.*1563 and converted into rooms in 1775. Oxford, king Charles's capital, was a major fortress in the Civil War of 1642-46, ringed with the mightiest defences in the country, few traces of which can be seen above ground, although part of the Parliamentary siege-works are visible (*3*). In 1644 the city suffered a major accidental fire in which Butcherrow (now Queen Street) and Pennyfarthing Street (now Pembroke Street) were burnt down (*75*), to be rebuilt when peace came.

8

MAKING SENSE OF THE PAST
IN QUEEN ANNE
& GEORGIAN OXFORD

Anthony Wood's burial service at Merton chapel in 1695 was conducted by the college chaplain, John Poynter (1668-1758). Born at Alkerton in north Oxfordshire, Poynter died in Oxford 90 years later. His grandfather, a Puritan minister put in as canon of Christ Church, had been ejected at the Restoration in 1660. His father Theophilus (d. 1709), an Oxford surgeon, had operated on Wood in 1678, drilling two holes through his shoulder for reasons of health. When the century began Poynter was in his early thirties; during his long life he observed all the great building projects of the period; in old age in 1749 he wrote *Oxoniensis Academia*, a guide to the university, made up of lists of college heads, benefactors, 'curiosities' and 'customs', but with some penetrating comments. An antiquary and collector, Poynter wrote pamphlets and books on history, climate and archaeology (77). Many of his papers and much of his private museum survive. He knew Thomas Hearne (1678-1735), the great antiquary and diarist of St Edmund Hall, whose notebooks make it clear that he found Poynter exasperating and thought him pretty dim, particularly in archaeological and historical matters. Poynter lived in Oxford through an age remarkable for varied, enlightened and inventive architecture and constant building-works, and also for constant and vigorous, even violent, squabbles over politics and religion, then inseparably linked, and vicious infighting at elections in which graduates voted, parliamentary and other; until 1950 the university sent two members to the House of Commons. Only a few university and college posts were appointed by outsiders; most were elected, several so fiercely fought that several elections for college headships ended up in court. As well as this continuous civil war of words, spoken and written, in the common rooms and streets of Oxford, a war of printed words raged between London and Oxford. From 1714 to 1760 Oxford was opposed to the Whig government and often accused of treason, but held up a mirror to the nation critically and honestly.

The Out lines of the Chief Figures on y PAVEMENT

An ACCOUNT of
A
Roman PAVEMENT,
Lately found at
STUNSFIELD
I N
OXFORD-SHIRE,
Prov'd to be 1400 Years Old.

By *JOHN POINTER*, M. A. Chaplain
of *Merton College* in *Oxford*, and Rector of
Slapton in *Northampton-shire.*

Imprimatur,
BERN. GARDINER,
June 30. 1713. Vice-Canc. OXON.

OXFORD:
Printed by *Leonard Lichfield*, for *Anth. Peisley*
Bookseller: And are to be Sold by *J. Morphew,*
near *Stationer's Hall,* LONDON. 1713.

Price Six-Pence.

77 John Poynter's book on the Roman mosaic pavement at Stonesfield, frontispiece and
title-page, 1713

With most colleges dominated by Tories, Oxford was constantly criticised in
the press, which often called for reform. College fellows, waiting for seven or
ten years for a rich college living to fall vacant, enjoyed flouting and evading
the government and the press, cultivating old members and wealthy landowners to pay for grand new buildings. A key figure in this game, Dr George Clarke
(1661-1736), of Brasenose and All Souls, politician, virtuoso and benefactor,
advised on, designed or helped to pay for a fascinating group of buildings. He
left a large collection of his architectural plans to Worcester College, rather than
All Souls, his own college, so fed up was he with rows. His principal master-
mason, William Townesend (1676-1739), adapted and built some of Clarke's
designs and designed, advised on and built many more; many of his bills, letters
and account-books survive. Wren's chief assistant Nicholas Hawksmoor (1661-
1736) often took time off from his work at Blenheim to provide advice and
plans (78). The great building boom of the early eighteenth century is richly
documented and deserves several large volumes of its own.

Early in the century academics, politicians, architects and master-masons
dreamed of remodelling great areas of the city into a kind of new Rome. The
city fathers laid out a tiny, elegant, boldly classical piazza in 1709-10 at the
south-west corner of Carfax, making room for it by pulling down the Mermaid

Tavern, which they had owned since 1469. The city's leading master-masons, William Townesend and Bartholomew Peisley, who often worked in partnership and knew Hawksmoor well from working at Blenheim since 1705, were among the most prominent members of the council, which agreed a plan and appealed for funds in October 1709. Lord Abingdon of Rycote and Wytham, closest of local grandees, gave 50 guineas. Thomas Rowney, attorney and city MP, gave £50; another £50 came from William Lancaster, vice-chancellor and provost of Queen's College, 'that old hypocritical, ambitious, drunken sot' as Hearne charitably described him. Peisley took over the lease of the old Mermaid cellars beneath the new piazza, patched them up with new vaults where necessary and let them out for storing wine; his heirs and executors continued to renew the lease for another 60 years and the vaults survived intact until the 1930s. Parts of their walls must still remain beneath the roadway at Carfax (*colour plate 13c*). Peisley built the colonnade above the vaults (*27a*) and faced up the sides of the Fleur de Lys to the south and the house to the west in a simple baroque style. The city also replaced the old Eastgate with a new triumphal arch (*40a-b*), not quite like Hawksmoor's dream version. On 16 February 1711 the city council appointed 'viewers' to inspect the gate and, on 23 February, voted to rebuild it in a 'handsome and ornamentall' way, at city expense. The masons

78 The Clarendon Building, designed by Nicholas Hawksmoor and built by William Townesend in 1712-15, served as the university's printing works until 1831; as a grand entry or triumphal arch it expresses Hawksmoor's dreams of grandeur and the forceful ambition of William Lancaster, vice-chancellor, provost of Queens, 'Sly-Boots' or the 'Northern Bear'; it stands in the Town Ditch on immensely deep footings of stone robbed from Whitefriars (now Beaumont Street); the workmen there found burials, stained glass, glazed floor-tiles and coins

Peisley and Townesend were among the viewers who reported that 'no repair is possible' and no doubt one or other of them designed and built the new one, without Hawksmoor lending a hand.

Oxford has two particularly splendid buildings of this time, both designed to link remote northern provinces with Oxford and with London. Queen's College, founded in 1341 but totally rebuilt between 1671 and 1754, is a grand monument to two generations of ambitious Cumbrians, among them Lancaster (78), and their success in church and state. The Radcliffe Library, established under John Radcliffe's will of 1714 and built in 1737-49, is a spectacular advertisement for the benefits of an Oxford education, showing what a poor boy from Yorkshire can achieve if he comes south and becomes a fashionable doctor. The 'Camera', as James Gibbs's great rotunda has come to be called, was the final achievement of a great period of college and university expansion, not in student numbers, which were in decline, but in fine and varied architecture. A distinctive feature of Oxford architecture at this time is a central range with two wings, a Renaissance notion borrowed from sixteenth-century French architecture and widely adopted in Cambridge long before it was taken up here. There it can sometimes seem almost welcoming, with the wings reaching out towards you. The Oxford versions are never very welcoming, as the wings are joined by an off-putting, almost defensive, screen wall, or run backwards to enclose an inner court or garden. Queen's and All Souls have ornate main ranges with side ranges running forwards, with screen walls along the front to keep us out. New College and Oriel both have short ranges running towards a garden. Dr Clarke's plan for Worcester College had short rangs, fairly close together, running forward to the street and longer ranges, further apart, running back on the garden front.

As well as Hearne and Poynter, we should mention other local antiquaries. Francis Wise (1695-1767), son of a prosperous Oxford mercer, was born in High Street, and educated at New College School, then from 1710 at Trinity College, where he was elected a fellow in 1718. He was appointed sub-librarian of the Bodleian in 1719 and, to help make ends meet, did some tutoring, one of his first pupils being Francis North (1704-90), later MP for Banbury, third Lord North and first earl of Guilford, father of Lord North, the unpopular politician whose advice to George III played a part in losing the American colonies. Wise advised him to study antiquities on the grand tour, 'triumphal arches, acqueducts, theatres and amphitheatres, columns, statues, busts &c'. In 1722 he published an edition of Asser's *Life of Alfred the Great* and in 1726 was elected keeper of the university archives and became curate-in-charge of Elsfield. He studied Waylands Smithy and the White Horse at Uffington and published pamphlets suggesting that the horse was a monument to Alfred's victory over the Danes in 871. In 1749, perhaps as 'a safe pair of hands', he was appointed the first Radcliffe Librarian, and for the next two decades discouraged both books and readers. In 1750 he published a decent catalogue of coins at the Bodleian Library, all now at the Ashmolean Museum. With a group of friends Wise played a memorable and rather malicious prank on the great antiquary Hearne in June 1723 (*79*). They got George Vertue (1684-1756), engraver to the Society of Antiquaries, to produce a single-sheet guide of a sort that were printed locally to sell to tourists to Old Sarum and such sites. Vertue was often in Oxford on business about the annual Almanacs, which he designed for the university from 1723 to 1751, each showing actual or proposed college buildings and relevant founders or benefactors, rather than the allegorical scenes popular before. Hearne had found, just to the west of Hythe Bridge, a small seventeenth -century alehouse, 'Dick Whittington and his Cat' or 'The Hole in the Wall', and had taken to meeting his friends there, country squires keen on local antiquities, wealthy Christ Church undergraduates who collected Roman coins, and most of the city's skilled printers, compositors, typefounders and binders. Hearne got on well with all of them, as a poor country boy who had been taken up by his local squire and sent to school and on to Oxford, becoming 'architypographus' (a post to do with printing) and janitor and then sub-librarian (1712-16) at the Bodleian Library, but was deprived for refusing to swear allegiance to George I. Wise and Vertue contrived an illustrated 'archaeological' guide to the little suburban alehouse which, because of Hearne and his friends, had gained a third name 'Antiquity Hall'. Across the top Vertue's print shows three small views: the first is a plan of a 'mosaic' pavement, the main room of the alehouse laid in pebbles and knucklebones, not Roman but typically seventeenth-century; the second shows the 'Propylæum' the narrow gate or 'Hole in the Wall' on Hythe Bridge Street which led to the alehouse; and the third shows a supposed wall-painting of three merry printers 'to be depicted opposite to ye Windows' dancing arm-in arm in front of the Sheldonian Theatre and their newly-completed press (*78*). The main scene at the bottom shows the alehouse as a major historic monument, with letters as signposts: E is 'The Manner of Entring' or front gate, shown cut-away, as it appears in the centre view of the top register, and B, the cottage itself, is 'The Mansion House' and so on. The title and relevant heraldry appear between top and bottom views on fluttering ribbons around a shield of arms fit to be carried into battle. In mock-heraldic terms 'the Antient Arms belonging to this Hall are *arg 3 Diota propr*', that is a white shield with three black-glazed drinking mugs of a familiar type of *c*.1670-1720. The right-hand ribbon explains that this is 'a Vessel to drink out of a Certain Liquer by ye Antients Call'd Zythium, by ye Modern Antiquarians called μιλδαλε' (mild ale, spelt in Greek). Hearne was not at all amused, calling the images and captions 'very silly ridiculous things & words in it... very much laugh'd at by all People, who cannot but look upon it as one of the weakest things ever done'. But it tells us a great deal amount about Georgian attitudes to the past and to each other. Wise spent much of his time embellishing his garden at Elsfield (*80*) with 'a triumphal arch, the tower of Babel, a Druid temple, and an Ægyptian pyramid' and other such agreeable fancies.

The Plan of the Hall, with the Tesellated Floor.

α. the Door   It a great Slab or Fire Stone
B. y.ᵉ Chimney 2 foot high. δ. Windoᵗ Each 1 foot w̄

Propylæum or hole in y.ᵉ Wall the Entrance to Antiquity Hall

arg: 3 Dict ad prop:

Typographicæ.   to be depicted on y.ᵉ inside of y.ᵉ Hall, opposite to y.ᵉ Windows.

the Antient Arms belonging to this Hall

a Vessel to drink out of y.ᵉ Certain Liquor by y.ᵉ Antients Calld

by y.ᵉ Modern Antiquarians call

ANTIQVITY HALL
Suburbanū: Oxon.

A. The Hall.
B. The Mansion House.
C. The Zythepsarium behind y.ᵉ House

D. The Way leading to y.ᵉ Hall.
E. The Manner of Entring
F. One waiting For Company.

G. The Stone Seats at y.ᵉ Door.
H. a Stone Wall for Enclosesure.

79 'Antiquity Hall', a quiet alehouse on Hythe Bridge Street. *G. Vertue, print, 1723*

80 Francis Wise's garden at Elsfield. *Print, 1750*

William Fletcher (1739-1826), son of a bookseller in the Turl, was a sickly child brought up a few miles north of the city at Yarnton, where the William Fletcher primary school keeps his name alive. Apprenticed to a draper in High Street opposite University College, he became a Freeman in 1765 and set up in business as a draper at 93 High Street, now part of the Old Bank Hotel. Until a dozen years ago this was Barclays' regional head office, the 'Old Bank', whose cheques always carried the alternative pre-Barclays name 'Fletcher, Parsons, Thomson' to honour its founding senior partner William Fletcher and his colleagues who, from the 1770s, prospered more from handling money than from selling sheets and cloth. Some members of the banking families were notable: Sir John Thomson (1908-99), chairman of Barclays 1962-73, introduced the credit card, and compared picking bank managers to judging racehorses. Fletcher himself, the city's leading banker, a bachelor and evangelical, was a great antiquary and collector of Oxford relics. He lies buried in Yarnton church in a medieval stone coffin from Godstow beneath a mock-medieval brass showing him in alderman's robes, with the inscription:

Yarnton, my childhood's home!
Do thou receive
This parting gift –
My dust to thee I leave.

Some of his collections surround him in the church, the medieval alabaster carved panels set in the wall behind the altar (*colour plate 7e*) and the stained glass in many of the windows. His diaries and extra–illustrated local books are in the Bodleian Library; old carved wooden posts and painted panels which he set up in his house in Broad Street are in the Museum of Oxford; and the door said to have confined the martyrs Cranmer, Ridley and Latimer in Bocardo, the city prison over Northgate, can be seen in St Michael's tower beside the former gate.

Another keen antiquary, Daniel Harris (1761-1840), was, like Fletcher, not an academic. This expert artist, architect, builder, water-engineer, and prison-keeper, kept up his simultaneous careers for much of his life in the parish of St Peter the Bailey. His prisoners in the county gaol were kept busy building locks to make the Thames more navigable. From an archaeological perspective, his most interesting achievement was to rebuild the crypt of St George's in the castle in a pastiche Romanesque style in 1794. He recorded the old crypt (*17a, lower and 17b, lower*), and then took it down, saving its four free-standing columns. On the same site he then built a larger new crypt, as an undercroft at the end of one of the new prison wings and, no doubt, as a bit of fun too. With two new stumpy columns, his complete 'fake' is rather more ornate than the real one had been, with wall-pilasters all round to carry the ribs; in the original the ribs of the groin-vault died into the walls.

9

REGENCY & VICTORIAN TIMES
& Dr ACLAND

In the nineteenth century Oxford was the home of giants, men of over-whelming personality, immense stature and towering achievement, household names for decades after their deaths. To understand the period we must visit a haunting and magical building quite unlike any other ever built, the University Museum of 1855-60, now the 'Oxford University Museum of Natural History'. I have known it, fascinated and puzzled at Christmas lectures as a small boy in the early 1940s, and on countless later visits. One of the world's great buildings, with a collection of international standing, the museum serves much of its original purpose as a market-place where scientists can display their wares for us to wonder at. To enter, or simply to approach, this fantastic won-derland, much of its rich carved decoration still unfinished, is just like being in a dream. It is an intensely satisfying, well-planned building with crisp chunky details of stone and, on the inside, brick, iron (both cast and wrought), and glass, still serving its original purpose to perfection. The Gothic design (83, 84, colour plate 11b) was a brilliant leap of imagination by the Irish architect Benjamin Woodward, not copied or borrowed from any one example or style, but combining motifs and details from many places. The blend of style and detail did not lead to a new understanding of medieval Europe, nor did the structural ironwork of its internal glass-roofed court make any contribution to engineering knowledge; rather the reverse, as the first version started to col-lapse under its own weight. Its other main function as a centre for scientific teaching and research has gradually moved out into new buildings and depart-ments all around, each of them a stage where leading scientists can perform like prima donnas in an opera, as they do. With a glazed internal courtyard 32.5m square, flanked by two storeys of cloisters on all four sides, with ranges of offices and lecture-rooms on the north, west and south, the museum mea-sures 55m north to south by 51m. The glass roof had to be high enough on the inside, more than 5.5m from the floor, to clear the stuffed giraffe brought

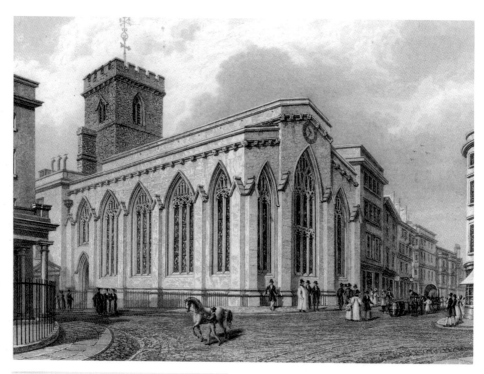

E.w. of Carfax Tower, showing the old roof-lines — Aug 26. 1897

81a-b a) *Above* St Martin's church, Carfax, as rebuilt by Plowman and Harris, 1820-22.
b) *Left* Manning's drawing of the tower with three old roof lines, various windows and openings, and the western nave pillars, 26 August 1897, before T.G. Jackson's 'restoration' *(colour plate 13b)*

82 Opposite The Botanic Garden in 1856; to the right of the gate is the residence of Professor Daubeney, who evaded Acland's attempt to move all the sciences to the Museum

from the old Ashmolean Museum. It had semi-attached annexes, a chemical laboratory in the form of a medieval kitchen to the south, and an anatomy yard to the north; three detached dwellings, a curator's house to the south-east (*69e*) and lodges to north-west and south-west, all now demolished; and several other detached buildings such as a macerating room for the anatomists and an observatory. With its excessively steep-pitched roofs and peculiar smells, seen by one commentator as a 'a Cathedral of science, fostering the study of nature as part of divine revelation', and by another as a 'bizarre and illogical building', the museum has reminded me since childhood of Paddington Station with its vast glass roof, funny smells and sense of excitement. Like a Renaissance palace or chapel, the museum is a classic example of how a patron, his advisers and builders can create an imperishable monument, in this case to all the arts and sciences, and to all its creators and their professional forebears.

The style and character of the museum mirror one of the great personalities of the nineteenth century, Henry Wentworth Acland (1815-1901), Oxford's most successful physician, a leading scientific activist involved in many aspects of city life. Born in 1815, the fourth of seven sons of a wealthy West Country squire, he was educated at Harrow, which he did not enjoy, and Christ Church in 1835-40. After a long 'gap year', from July 1837 to May 1839, he achieved a pass degree, having spent his time away in Rome and aboard HMS *Pembroke*, commanded by a family friend, cruising round the Mediterranean making notes and drawings of the landscapes, ancient ruins and the Turkish court. After

83 The University Museum of 1855-60 (*colour plate 11b*), from an 1859 newspaper; fitting out went on until 1866; the carving and decoration were never finished

studying medicine at St George's Hospital and in Edinburgh, he was summoned back to Oxford to take up a specialist college post, as Dr Lee's Reader in Anatomy at Christ Church in 1846. He bought the house and practice of a leading city physician and became the most influential scientist in the university, as he remained for the next half century. He was appointed physician to the Radcliffe Infirmary in 1847, followed by a string of other posts, as Professor of Clinical Medicine, Radcliffe librarian and, most prestigious of all, Regius Professor of Medicine 1858-94. In 1847 many leading scientists assembled in Oxford for a week-long meeting of the British Association for the Advancement of Science; Acland, as organising secretary, arranged evening meetings in the Clarendon Building (*78*) opposite his house in Broad Street. E.B. Pusey, Regius Professor of Hebrew and most influential of high churchmen, invited him to put up some of the eminent visitors in his lodgings at Christ Church while he was away. At the end of the week Acland drafted a proposal for 'an edifice... with one or more lecture-rooms' to house a library and the collections scattered round Oxford, not least the geological and mineralogical specimens in the Clarendon Building. In 1848 he issued a pamphlet about 'furtherance of knowledge in Anatomy, Botany, Chemistry, Natural Philosophy Geology, &c'. In that year Cambridge started a natural science tripos and Oxford at once followed suit, voting to set up the School of Natural Science in 1849. Always in the centre of the action, Acland had a happy knack of being on both sides of every fence at once, closely linked to the low-church 'Clapham Sect' through his mother, Sarah Hoare of the wealthy banking family, and with many high-church friends. In 1849 Acland assembled an ad-hoc committee meeting in the warden's lodgings at New College, a college which had steered well clear of proposals for reform, to urge that 'a building should be erected' for specimens and study of the natural sciences to be housed 'under one roof'. The vice-chancellor in 1850 was F.C. Plumptre, master of University College in 1836-70, an enthusiast at making plans and supervising building work at his college and elsewhere: he had chaired the low-church committee which built the Martyrs' Memorial as a Protestant statement against the Tractarians and as a Gothic counterblast against the classical style of the University Galleries. Finding by chance that the press had a surplus of £60,000, Plumptre proposed to spend half of it on Acland's new museum and laboratories for natural science. Pusey led the high-church protesters who claimed that money made from the Scriptures should not be spent on scientific investigations which might undermine them; but a few years later, in 1854, the high-church vote produced a decisive majority for the museum, after Acland's honesty and humour had gained Pusey's support. Both younger sons of wealthy country squires, Pusey's brother Philip, an MP and leading agricultural reformer who had arranged the display of farm machinery at the Great Exhibition in 1851, is said to have suggested the museum's glass-roofed courtyard. Acland skilfully manipulated the Hebdomadal Board (the university's governing council consisting of all heads of colleges, one of whom, as vice-chancellor, was chief executive), and Convocation (the superior body comprising all Masters of Arts, resident and absentee, which elected the university's two members of parliament after prolonged and fiery campaigns and also voted on many academic appointments and final decisions).

As rail networks expanded in the 1840s and '50s the absentees came more often to vote in person. The national press delighted in relating how issues, constantly blurred by tensions between London and Oxford, were affected by parliamentary politics, high-church and low-church differences, and rival bands of reformers seeking to shake up the syllabus and redefine the meaning of liberal education, make the natural sciences an academic subject, and help poorer students (issues still today being aired on television, at Westminster and in the press). Threats of government-enforced change seemed and were very real. Some men distrusted change for its own sake and tried to keep out Catholics, Jews, Nonconformists and politicians. Some colleges did their best to stay clear of interference and reform by other Oxford academics and outside bodies. There was no lavish government funding; but some professors and readers were appointed and paid by the state, extra funds coming sometimes in rather odd ways. In 1825 the eminent geologist, William Buckland (1784-1856), could barely manage on his three salaries, as fellow of Corpus Christi, as reader in mineralogy and as reader in geology, both crown appointments; Lord Grenville (1759-1834), nominal head of the university as chancellor, asked his political associate Lord Liverpool, the prime minister, to make Buckland a canon of Christ Church, another crown appointment, to help him with his research expenses travelling round Europe collecting stones. Geology, then a rave subject, no longer commands quite such clout. With a small investment income, less than that of some colleges, the university had to maintain and staff one

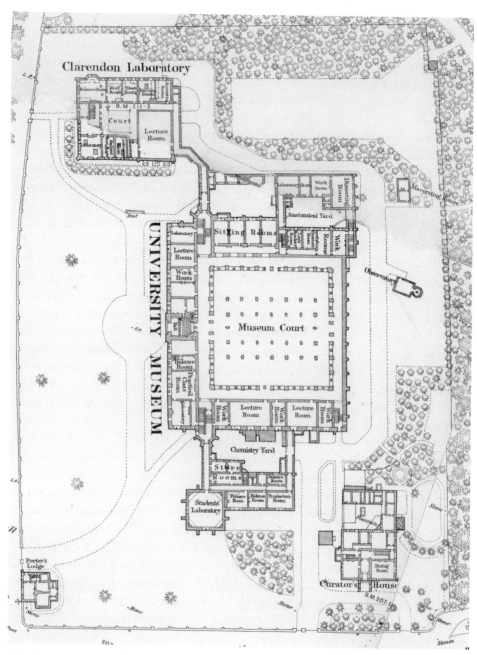

Clarendon Laboratory

Balance Room · Heat Room · Electric Room · Room
B.M. 211·3
Court
Laboratory · Lecture Room

UNIVERSITY MUSEUM

Laboratory · Sitting Rooms
Lecture Room
Work Room
Museum Hall
Balance Room
Practical Class
Laboratory

Laboratory Stores · Work Room · Dissecting Room
Anatomical Yard
Room · Room
Room · Work Room

Museum Court

Observatory

Macerating House

Work Room · Lecture Room · Work Room · Lecture Room · Work Room

Chemistry Yard

Store Rooms
Furnace Room · Balance Room · Prælector's Room
Students' Laboratory

Fountain

Store

Dining Room

Curator's House
B.M. 207·

Porter's Lodge

Stones

84 The University Museum and Clarendon Laboratory for physics, added in 1868–70. *Ordnance Survey 1/500 map*

group of older buildings, the Bodleian Library, the Examination Schools, the Sheldonian Theatre and the Ashmolean Museum then in Broad Street, and another group of newer ones, the Taylorian Library and the University Galleries in Beaumont Street, now part of the Ashmolean Museum. The university, almost by chance, was fabulously rich in the 1850s, owning and running the city's major industry, the Press, a printing and publishing business which produced two kinds of books, all badly printed on poor paper. The 'learned' books, interesting or not, were barely marketed, but bibles, in those days, sold by the hundreds of thousands and made vast profits. In 1826-30 the delegates of the Press splashed out on grandiose buildings and paid £30,000 for their new premises in Walton Street, designed by Daniel Robertson (a raffish Scot who fled to Ireland for unexplained reasons) to look like Buckingham Palace. In 1841-5 the delegates gave £33,000 for the University Galleries designed by C.R. Cockerell, and still found themselves in 1850 with a large surplus. Over the next decade they were able to hand over about £10,000 a year to the university and, as late as 1876-82, they paid much of the cost, £100,000 or so, of the Examination Schools. On 17 May 1881, publication day of the *Revised New Testament*, this profitable and rewarding link of business with Holy Scripture reached a climax, when the Press sold a million copies in one day, leading to over-production, over-capacity and all such financial ills. By then the well-endowed colleges, the old aristocracy and wealthy country squires all found their incomes shrinking as farm tenants suffered from cheap imported grain in arable areas and sheep-blight on pastoral land.

Acland and the other founders of the museum intended it to be the focus of all the natural sciences. As Oxford already had plenty of skins, bones and stones to display, they decided to bring them together within a geological-cum-botanical display. The interior courtyard's two-storey cloister (*colour plate 11b*) has 125 lesser columns with polished shafts, each a specimen of a different kind of stone, each capital carved with plant-details. They also designed it, like a Valhalla, to be a monument to great men of science. The 33 rectangular piers of the lower storey have corbelled plinths to support near-life-size statues, of which 18 were installed in the nineteenth century: a random collection of three ancient Greeks, a medieval friar, four foreigners, five Cambridge men, two Oxford men, two great engineers (Watt and Stephenson) and the dissenter Joseph Priestley. The general effect is uninspiring and the Cambridge men, perhaps accidentally, all look ridiculous; Darwin wears a thick cloak for fear of catching cold, and Newton tries to avoid hostile glares from his rival Leibnitz. Acland quite never managed to round up all the sciences. Botany, now called 'Plant Sciences', developed out of medicine, but remained a conspicuous absentee from Acland's project; the professor C.G.B. Daubeny (1795-1867) agreed to transfer his plants from the Botanic Gardens (*82*) to a new site by the museum, but never got around to doing so. For over half a century, from October 1847 until he died in October 1901, Acland lived in the very centre of academic life at 40 Broad Street. His house, built partly of stone in the seventeenth century, partly of lath-and-plaster in the eighteenth and nineteenth, was one of a dozen large, mostly timber-framed houses torn down in 1937 to make room for the New Bodleian Library. At first it had a dozen or so rooms, but Acland enjoyed altering, extending and tinkering with it, adding and altering the next door houses, Nos 39 and 41, to make it a vast rambling place with 30 rooms, to hold his family of seven sons and two daughters together with many servants and a flood of guests. In 1857 he added a brick library designed by Benjamin Woodward, architect of the museum; he also owned another two neighbouring houses which he could take over if he ever needed the space. By the end of his long and active life the extended house had a frontage of 16.5m; the 30 rooms were packed with paintings, drawings, prints and other mementoes; with the garden, stables and coachman's cottage it was 69m deep.

One other Oxford scientist lived in a house designed by Woodward, while two more emulated Acland's library by adding rooms designed by Woodward to their houses. John Phillips, first keeper of the museum, lived in the Curator's House (*69e, 83-4*); his bust stands in the museum. In 1858-59 Bartholomew Price, Sedleian Professor of Natural Philosophy, added a tall brick back wing to 11 St Giles; its steeply-pitched roof makes the link with the museum very clear. In 1862 the chemistry professor Sir Benjamin Brodie added a wing to his box-like Georgian villa, Cowley Place, now part of St Hilda's College. These distinctive extended houses were characteristic of scientists; not to be left out, Acland's old tutor Henry Liddell, dean of Christ Church, persuaded his college to employ the firm (lacking Woodward's special genius as he had died), to build a range of rooms, Meadow Buildings of 1863-66 (*colour plate 11a*). Acland played a distinguished part in improving the city's public health. He made a special study of the poorest suburbs of St Aldate's, St Clements, St Ebbe's, St Thomas's and Jericho, which had suffered most in three major cholera epidemics, and campaigned tirelessly for better drains and water. He published plans, sections and elevations (a pioneering study of vernacular housing) of the back-to-back cottages in Gas Street, St Ebbe's, where there had been 11 cases of cholera in 1854, the worst of the outbreaks. The back-to-backs with two three-storey cottages, 14 rooms sharing a single pump and privy, had been built of brick in the 1820s on a building-plot 7.5m wide and 25m deep, less than one hundredth the size of the museum site.

During the nineteenth century Oxford changed remarkably. In 1800 the city was very compact and had hardly expanded beyond the limits it had reached in the 1270s. In the first Census of 1801 the population of the 14 city parishes, with St Clements, was 10,936, rising to 27,843 in 1851. By 1901, with hundreds more streets and thousands more houses, the built-up area reached for a mile or so in every direction that the rivers allowed. The population of the Municipal Borough was 49,285, while the Parliamentary Borough, with slightly different boundaries, had 49,336 inhabitants. With very

85 A private house for only 14 years, No.17 Norham Gardens was designed by F. Codd (*38b*) for Mr W. Aldridge in 1873-4; in 1888-1916 it was occupied by St Hugh's Hall (now College), a women's college which extended it, right, in 1891-2. For two generations it was a theological college, St Stephen's House, and it is now an annexe of St Edmund Hall

little industry, certainly no heavy industry, there were five times as many people in Oxford in 1901 as there had been 100 years before. Everybody and everything went by train, as it had not in 1801, or by horse, as it always had. The centre of a prosperous farming area and a transport hub in the days of turnpike roads and mail coaches, and to a lesser extent of horse-drawn barges on rivers and canals, the city's population grew faster in the first half of the century than in the second, when the wider spread of railways allowed the major industrial regions of the Midlands and the North easier and faster connections. Some of the early suburban developments, like Summertown, were well outside the old built-up area and should be visited by bicycle. At the top of Headington Hill we can walk round the narrow lanes of an ambitious, almost unknown, development of the 1820s, which seems to have no name and no street-names. T.P. Cox, militia quartermaster, and G.J. Gardner, a painter of St Clements, paid £1,500 for a field there and divided it into 54 house-plots with two access lanes. At auction on 18 April 1825 they sold 21 plots for a total of £1,268 and were left with 33 unsold plots. One of the partners, Gardner, had borrowed £600 for his share of the venture, and went bankrupt. During the next 50 years ten houses were built, while most of the area became private gardens and orchards. The city's richest family, the Morrells of Headington Hill Hall, on the other side of the main

86 The King Alfred memorial fountain planned for Broad Street in 1859 by John Gibbs, sculptor, writer and architect, who designed some striking North Oxford houses and Banbury Cross; work began but it was never put up

road, and Morrells Brewery in St Thomas's, gradually acquired all but one of the properties. To the east they had a large walled kitchen garden and a training school for domestic servants. Most of the city's new streets and houses were built, more succesfully, as speculations, without any coherent master-plan. The city had gas streetlights by 1819, filtered mains water in 1854-84, and new drains in 1873-80, services not at once visible but essential for Oxford's domestic, commercial and academic worlds.

All the historic colleges, except All Souls, carried out ambitious building-schemes in stone, mostly new ranges of rooms which we can see all round the centre of the city (*46-7*). Oxford's favourite architect, Thomas Graham Jackson (1835-1924), left his own flamboyant and distinctive mark on the university, the colleges and the city. His senior cousins were squires at Duddington in north Northamptonshire, where the parish church is full of their monuments; they were also land agents in the nearby town of Stamford in south Lincolnshire. Educated at the newly founded Brighton College and in 1854-8 at Wadham, Jackson was articled to George Gilbert Scott, most successful of all Victorian architects, whose office in Spring Gardens, Westminster, with 30 pupils, assistants and clerks, all enthusiastic Goths, churned out hundreds of new churches, repaired old ones by the dozen, and had almost a monopoly of Cathedral restoration. Scott was a competent observer, prone to rip out late-medieval or Tudor windows and replace them with replicas of Norman or early Gothic ones, of which he could see traces. One of his assistants, J.T. Irvine, usually working on site as a clerk of works, was the best church archae-ologist of the age. In 1861 Jackson set up on his own, keeping his links with Scott, and led a congenial life without many commissions but plenty of time for study abroad. Scott restored the nave of Ketton church in Rutland, but left the chancel for Jackson to restore, as it lay just across the Welland from Duddington. In 1864 Jackson became a prize fellow at Wadham, which gave him a base in Oxford without requiring residence, while his Ketton work led to commissions at Uppingham in Rutland and at other public schools, and a reputation for educational work. In 1876, after much debate and several changes of mind, the university gave Jackson a great breakthrough, choosing his competition design for the Examination Schools in High Street. Unlike all the other entries, which were Gothic, his winning design was drawn from such Elizabethan and Jacobean prodigy houses as Burghley, near Stamford, and Kirby, not far from Duddington. This seemed to give Oxford a new mix of styles, already reassuringly familiar from the Schools Quadrangle (72), the Fellows Quad at Merton (52) and Wadham itself, but more assertive than any real Jacobean buildings. Knowing that two schemes had been chosen and rejected, Jackson persuaded his committee to start work on the foundations while he made detailed drawings and the 'quantities were being taken out'. This led to most interesting, if aborted, archaeological discoveries.

The university itself was involved almost continuously from the 1820s to the 1890s in planning and building, to provide itself with five striking and monumental buildings and many lesser ones. The Press, its first great project (p.167), was a great commercial success which allowed the university to build most of the others without having to bother the patrons or benefactors who could readily have been found at that time. In 1800 the university decided to hold written examinations, copied from Chinese civil service practice. Wracked with agonising debates about reform and religion, Oxford remained for decades the nation's training-ground for careers in church and state without expanding, largely ignoring its younger sister at Cambridge, its cousins, Trinity College Dublin and the four Scottish universities, and its second cousins, the successful long-established dissenting academies. In the second half of the century the city's growth slowed but the university grew faster and changed more. Some of Oxford's great Victorians, Pusey, Liddell and Acland, were younger sons of country gentlemen. Others, like Jowett and Ruskin, were the sons of London tradesmen, a furrier and a rich art-loving wine-merchant; Stubbs was the orphan son of a Yorkshire solicitor, Dodgson

87 Henry Taunt (1842-1922), the city's leading commercial photographer, left over 53,000 superb glass–plate negatives showing scenes of all kinds of Oxford and elsewhere; in 1924-5 a far-sighted city librarian paid less than £100 for several thousand negatives, prints and papers; this view, not in the library collection, shows a branch at No.41 High Street, briefly occupied by Taunt in the 1890s

(Lewis Carroll) the son of a Cheshire vicar. Their contemporaries, well aware of their confidence and ceaseless activity, felt that 'there has never been a time when Oxford was richer in men of large views, boundless energy and powers of work, and possessing clear ideas both of what they wanted and of how to compass it.' At the end of the Victorian period, Acland saw the beginning of a golden age of pleasure in 1885-1914 for the academic families in the centre of the city and its growing northern suburb; their memoirs tell us of those lost times.

Much of Oxford's Victorian architecture was produced as a symbol of triumph in some now long-forgotten controversy; but, however hard we try, we cannot recognise any distinctive style or type of building or architect actively working for the 'Diehards' or 'Reformers', 'Tractarians' or 'Evangelicals'. At Pembroke College the radical reforming low-churchman Francis Jeune, master from 1843, was banned for a few weeks in almost eighteenth-century style. When he took office he increased student numbers, embarked on an ambitious building programme, and set about changing all the rules with gusto, altering not only the statutes of his own college, but also, in time, those of the university itself. His best monument is the imposing north range of the garden quad, the handsome new dining hall, and the master's lodgings. Nonconformist colleges moved to Oxford and gave themselves handsome stone buildings as near the centre as possible, in a Gothic style. Four new womens' colleges took a different approach, settling further from the centre in large family houses (*85*) or building in brick in a modified Georgian style with sash windows. The one completely new Victorian college for men, Keble, is brick and has sash windows, but the style chosen was the most extreme and colourful Gothic.

In the 1850s the University Museum gave our knowledge of Oxford's past an unexpected bonus; the geologist John Phillips looked down the foundations and found some Roman coins. The museum proved to have been sited astride the city's great earthwork defences of the Civil War in 1642-6, so that the foundations had to be dug much deeper, and cost much more than anticipated. As scientific departments and laboratories have sprung up round the museum, all kinds of prehistoric burials, ring-ditches, Roman features and furtherlengths of Civil War ditch have been recorded. Acland himself was responsible for an immense amount of digging (one report on which, W.H.White's *Main Drainage of Oxford*, an informative study of the city's archaeology, was the first printed book I ever read in the Bodleian Library). In 1876 at the Examination Schools, T.G. Jackson's clerk of works was Robert Edwards 'a Welshman, a very intelligent man with tastes and knowledge of geology and antiquities far beyond his station', who embarked on a large-scale open-area excavation, reported in some detail in the national press. Many late Saxon finds came to light, such as pottery, spindlewhorls, a gold ring, a finely carved stone. Edwards must have made detailed records and drawn plans and sections, as Irvine had established as standard practice on Scott's more prestigious jobs. There was plenty of time and money; it was to be over a year before contracts were signed in August 1877 and the Press had its usual huge surplus. For some reason the science lobby opened fire on the operation, perhaps fearing to lose funding for new laboratories and equipment. The anatomy professor George Rolleston claimed that the features uncovered were not pit-dwellings, but merely gravel pits, a tragic misjudgement, as Rolleston was himself a keen archaeologist. He had excavated Roman pottery-kilns at Sandford, on land belonging to his friends, the Morrells of the brewery and Headington Hill Hall. He had worked on the Roman and Saxon cemetery at Frilford and collected burials dug up in the medieval town, primarily in search of skulls. He built up a varied collection for his professional work, only to be bitterly satirised in 1878 for his wide interests in 'Saxon inter-ments, early ceramic ware, and prehistoric pigs'. We must hope that Edwards's records will come to light, perhaps in a roll of tracing-paper from some other project, and that we may be able to recognise large and small cellar-pits (*12-14*), perhaps even a lost church. In his many later Oxford

88 An undergraduate room at Christ Church, Peckwater 2.12. *R.W. Buss, print, 1842*

buildings Jackson lost his interest in archaeology, but continued his own researches in architectural and college history.

Among my many second-hand memories of Victorian Oxford, I vividly recall an afternoon in November 1954. I was sitting in my college rooms (*88-9*), heard a timid knock on the door and called 'Come in'. A dear old man, who must have been in his eighties, came in and asked if he could look round. He told me that 'I had these rooms in '94' and went on to recognise my dining table, my chaise longue, and my elegant mid-Victorian armchair, all of them pushed to the back and effectively replaced by later, duller sofas and armchairs. 'I had that, and that, and that', he told me. I hope I gave him a cup of tea, but alas, with the carelessness of youth, I never asked his name or noted it down or asked him for any further details about his time in my rooms. To a slight extent I paid homage to him, and to all our predecessors, on my last night there in June 1956, when I gave a dinner-party for 12. We sat round my Regency or early Victorian dining table, for once assembled from its component parts, and feasted off a standard menu from the kitchen served by my scout, who patiently dashed up and down in the intervals from other much grander functions.

89a-f This Page and Overleaf An undergraduate room at Christ Church, Peckwater 2.12 with D.J. Roaf, maths scholar of the House. *Photo, 1955*

10

THE TWENTIETH CENTURY

Oxford, most beautiful of cities when I was young and there was no traffic, no tourists and almost no students, is now grossly congested and polluted by greed and folly. How could so many clever men have failed to halt this subtle and relentless progress? Far too many people push their way through the streets. Two million tourists a year come to Oxford, most of them just for a few hours; if the city is ever to become habitable again, they must be actively discouraged. Education should be actively discouraged too, as 30,000 long-term students come for a year or two or three, with another 20–30,000 short-term students coming for a weekend or a month. At intervals over the last 50 years, as I recall, the city, the university, the colleges and even the tourist industry have all announced an end to their own active expansion; but none of them has been able to resist the dream of increased income and a drive for increased numbers. Oxford's second university, once the School of Art, later the 'Tech', the 'Poly', and now Oxford Brookes, was lately accused of taking more students without providing housing for them, thus putting pressure on the suburbs of Cowley and Marston, which have been taking in students for decades. Perhaps all forms of science should be rooted out and driven to the ring-road, or sold to Cambridge. The last century was a great time for Oxford myths. You should not believe anything that anybody tells you about anything, particularly not about Oxford. To explain something of the city's present state, I will relate two myths with some element of truth; the first really concerns the suburbs, but had an impact on the centre of the city. The second is about the centre, but had an impact on the suburbs.

'Ah, Mr Morris, I've been expecting you', said the banker Arthur Gillett in 1912 as he greeted William Morris, who ran a bicycle-repair and car-hire business, at the start of a crucial meeting that led to the vast growth and amazing transformation of Oxford during the last century. I have read and been told several versions of the story, and it is not altogether clear whether the meeting took place in Gilletts' main Oxford bank, now Barclays in Cornmarket, or in the Cowley Road branch. The humble Morris, who was to become Lord

Nuffield, our very own open-handed hypochondriac multi-millionaire, came away with a loan of £4,000, of Gillett's money, not the bank's. He was a partner in the bank, so it did not make all that much difference until he and his partners sold out to Barclays. Morris had already borrowed £4,000 from Lord Macclesfield to add to his own shilling. He went ahead and bought a disused military college at Cowley, a handy place to assemble motor cars. Oxfordshire, with Rutland, paid the lowest agricultural wages in England. James Mason of Eynsham Hall, the first man in the county to buy a motor car, using his mining fortune from Portugal, had lately ignored the protests of his fellow landowners and put up his labourers' wages from ten shillings (50p) a week to twelve and sixpence (62.5p). Morris knew that he could find workers glad of a regular wage. In the city until at least the 1950s a sizeable and obedient labour-pool of poorly paid college servants depended on undergraduates' tips. In the long summer vacations they had to go without or go away to find work at the seaside. Building workers were kept firmly in hand by the Oxford Master Builders' Association, which met regularly to keep wages down, share out contracts, and pass round the names of troublemakers to ensure that they would never work here again. Although Oxford was not industrialised to any extent there were skilled metal workers, most of them in two fair-sized engineering firms, Allen's at Cowley, which produced steam-rollers and steam-ploughs, but never tried motor cars, and Lucy's in Jericho, which made steel bookcases, lamp-posts and steam roller wheels for Allen's, and also at Gills the ironmongers.

From the 1920s to the 1980s, making and selling motor cars seemed to overtake Oxford's long-established 'word business', but this was a mirage like everything else about the place. Morris could never have foreseen that, when he needed labour in Oxford's boom years of the late 1920s and '30s, the Depression would send him a flood of out-of-work coal-miners from South Wales. Born of confronting managers and mine-owners, their attitudes created a new subject, Industrial Relations, which the university's extra-mural department was to exploit. By 1939 almost 12,000 people, including thousands of Welsh miners, worked in the twin factories, Morris Motors and Pressed Steel, at Cowley. By 1944 over 17,000 workers, among them very many women, were making tanks, training planes, jerricans, mines and other war products. They rebuilt damaged Spitfires and melted down crashed German bombers for scrap. Morris's staff, skilled at breaking down complex tasks into simple stages, allowed housemaids and shopgirls on his Cowley production-lines to make a naval torpedo in 135 woman-hours; before the war skilled dockyard craftsmen had taken almost 900 man-hours. Seen from the air at low-level, the illusionist camouflage which covered the works, fading slowly in the decades after the war, made them look like streets and houses. The intelligence officers of the Luftwaffe, studying high-level air photographs, cannot have been fooled, but simply failed to grasp the vast capacity and immense military value of the works, with their own railway and sidings, their own airfield, and, for field after field, a scrapyard full of crashed planes all plainly visible from the air; Oxford was never bombed. By the 1960s there were 30,000 workers at Cowley, by then notorious for strikes, walk-outs and trouble of every kind. There was a constant legend that many of the workers had built their cars at home from parts taken back in their lunchboxes, or wrapped in raincoats on the back of their bikes. Whenever the shift changed or there was a cry of 'Everybody out', a mass of workers on their bikes filled the Cowley Road, forcing all other traffic into the kerb. As production grew, the factories grew and Oxford grew; and the Master Builders decided quietly among themselves which sprawling new housing estate each would make his own.

In his lifetime William Morris, Lord Nuffield from 1938, gave away £27m to good causes, medical and local. He founded the Oxford college named for his title, a chair of Spanish, an orthopaedic centre, and a great charity for medical research. Seeming determinedly ordinary to some, he could make the most princely gestures. In 1936, as the university was ceremonially accepting his offer of £1.25m for a Medical School Trust, Sir William, as he had become, calmly stood up to ask if he might make it £2m. At the Encaenia Garden Party of the same year he met Christopher Chavasse, master of St Peter's Hall, then in a bad way for funding, and quietly told him to expect a cheque for £50,000 the following day. Morris was involved with many architects, and his own commercial buildings deserve more than a glance. In 1910 the local architects Tollit & Lee designed, on the site of the old stables where his motor business was beginning to grow, a new garage in Queen Anne style with a modest triumphal arch leading through to the workshops in which his first car was soon to be assembled. In 1980 the workshops were rebuilt as college rooms behind the quietly theatrical facade. In 1912 another local architect, H. Quinton, built Morris a showroom at 36-7 Queen Street in the city centre, with huge glass windows and a long passage from the street which allowed you to see the cars from front, side and back, with another show-room above, linked by a great car-lift. The front, with mullioned windows with leaded lights, topped by a half-timbered gable, encouraged dreams of the 'Open Road' and remote country places. It is now a restaurant, with no hint of quiet village tea-rooms three generations ago. In 1933 Morris Motors moved its sales and maintenance departments to new premises of imperial grandeur in St Aldate's, the old Grandpont, designed by H.W. Smith and built of gold stone with Corinthian pilasters and huge curving show-windows. They are now the Crown Courts (*colour plate 12*), far grander than modern purpose-built courts in Cambridge and elsewhere. The Cowley works themselves, the heart of Morris's empire, have been mostly pulled down and the earlier, showy late Victorian wings of the military college converted into flats. None of the good causes that Morris supported so generously built anything worthy of him. In 1934-5 he paid for Staircase 4 at St Peter's Hall (now College) as a memorial to his mother; like

Staircases 1–3 it is a late seventeenth-century pastiche in red brick, designed by a minor local architect R. Fielding Dodd, advised by Sir Herbert Baker, without much imagination. In 1937-8 for the parish of Cowley he built the district church of St Luke, which towers over the old military college, designed by Harold Rogers, a City alderman but not a great architect. Father Beauchamp, vicar of Cowley, was astonished when he realised the scale of the church; fortunately the nave is hidden by the storage-floors of the Oxfordshire Archives which has taken it over, to the relief of the Church of England. Morris, or Nuffield as he had become, tried to encourage an interest in technology and hoped that his Oxford college would turn out like the Massachusetts Institute of Technology, but he was outwitted by academic bureaucrats who rephrased his ideas to favour political and economic studies. He would sometimes, paternally, refer to his college as 'that bloody Kremlin'. The architect, Austen Harrison (1891-1976), chosen by a university committee in 1938, had worked only in northern Greece and Palestine and came up with a vaguely Near Eastern design, to be faced in stark white Portland stone. The committee approved but Lord Nuffield was horrified and insisted on a new architect, or at least a completely new design, which he got. Carried out in 1948-60 in a half-baked neo-Cotswold style, which must have an impact on the college's intellectual prowess, it ensured that the architect did no other work in this country, and he retired to exile in the Mediterranean.

The second myth, which shows how central our local concerns are to national politics, just as if Oxford were part of Whitehall, concerns a Cabinet meeting called in July 1956 by Anthony Eden, Churchill's designated successor as prime minister. There were two items of supreme national importance on the agenda: the first, whether to drive a road through Christ Church Meadow as a bypass for the High Street; the second, whether to invade Egypt and reclaim the Suez Canal. After prolonged discussion, the cabinet, most of whom had been up at Christ Church, put off any decision about the first item and, as a casual afterthought, agreed by a brief show of hands to attack Egypt secretly with France and Israel. My tutors were horrified by this shocking and illegal action. I thought it was all rather fun, not realising how it would weaken our failing credibility in the Mediterranean and the Near East, as if that mattered while the fate of the Meadow was at stake. This row went on for years with endless repercussions. A similar battle, fought out in Oxford and Whitehall a little earlier, had ended less happily and sealed the fate of the city centre, at the same time providing me with a useful technical education (pp.29-37). In 1953 Harold Macmillan, minister of housing and local government, had been put forward for an honorary doctorate, as a Balliol man, a senior cabinet minister, and a businessman with a large share of the celebrated family publishing business. Woolworths had bought a shabby Georgian building, the Clarendon Hotel in Cornmarket, to pull it down and build a giant store. Under new planning legislation, the city, backed by the university, had refused permission, fearing that increased shop-pers and traffic would make central Oxford more crowded and intolerable than it already was in the early 1950s. Woolworths appealed and Macmillan reversed the city's decision in favour of big business. A faction of Oxford dons, appalled by this threat to civilised life and the increased traffic that would result, threatened to vote against the honorary degree, and Macmillan's nomination was quietly withdrawn. A few years later he became Prime Minister, the celebrated 'Supermac' with his 'wind of change' and, soon after, chancellor of the university, a post he filled with dignity, wit and aplomb for more than a quarter of a century. By then the damage was done and a precedent established for vast stores wrecking city centres everywhere. The result of Macmillan's decision was the largest single redevelopment in the city centre, which took place in 1955-6 (*12a-b*). The story is at once a farce, a tragicomedy and a real tragedy, as the shabby Georgian hotel turned out to be largely of *c*.1550, partly of *c*.1300 with a vaulted cellar in part at least of *c*.1100, which would have saved it, had this been known. But none of the city councillors opposed to the development, and none of their sup-porters among the dons, had bothered to examine the hotel and note obvi-ous signs of age, such as a high rubble wall on the north side and the uneven windows of the main street front. W.A. Pantin, tutor in medieval history at Oriel College, commented in 1958, when it was too late: 'Outwardly, the Clarendon seemed just a pleasant but rather undistinguished late Georgian building, so that it could be argued at the time of the discussions and inquiry about its demolition that it was not a building of historic or artistic impor-tance'. Pantin recorded the historic fabric above ground while it was being was pulled down (*69c*), and his record is all we have, as the old inn was com-pletely swept away, except for a few bits in museum stores, mainly re-cycled medieval carvings from some monastic site. We did not keep enough sample timbers to establish a date, or series of dates, from the tree-rings. Fifty years ago construction techniques were rudimentary; jib-cranes were in use but digging machines were not; the contractors hired Irish navvies to dig the foundation pits, so that conversations in Erse, strange half-English riddles, muttered plots against someone (I never knew whether it was the foreman, the English government, or me, a first-year student) accompanied spectacu-lar progress downward in each hole. After a weekend when, I read in the local paper, a military store 30 miles away was broken into and 50 army rifles taken, my favourite gang quietly evaporated like hobgoblins and never came back. I remember standing by the west end of the vaulted cellar as the junior at a meeting while E.M. Jope, just back from Belfast, the keeper of antiquities at the Ashmolean Museum and one of his assistant keepers, a job I was to succeed to four years later, discussed what to do next. I glanced down and picked up, from among many fragments of German stoneware, a large piece of coloured Venetian wine-glass of *c*.1600, to judge from my later acquaintance with that

e Clariſsimi viri Dⁿⁱ Christophori Wren
nomuä Saviliaũ, & Coll.omu. Anim. olim Socij. D e =
ij Regiæ Maj.tis per Uniuerſā Angliā Architecti Generalis.

90a A serious visitor of the sort to be encouraged at the Sheldonian Theatre. *Loggan, 1675*

kind of thing. I handed it round and the assistant keeper said: 'We've got plenty of *that*.' The keeper, a world expert on Roman glass, said: 'Yes', and threw it away. We were standing by a stone-lined pit which, as I now know, was perhaps 5m deep and stuffed with high-quality Jacobean glass and pottery. Discouraged, I made no attempt to investigate further. It may still be there, full of rare glass and pottery. That was my real education, rather than the 'more humane letters' that I was meant to be studying, the hours sitting in an airless hall listening to a nervous and self-important lecturer spouting high-flown words that might or might not make sense, and the hours reading page after page of the same kind of stuff, making notes on it and, worst of all, painfully and with many ink-blots, writing several pages of verbiage, to produce an argument supporting one view or the other, whether or not I knew anything about it or understood what I was doing. I never thought much of it as a formal education; but at least I was using the rest of my time

90b The horrors of tourism, to be discouraged. *Woodward & Cruikshank, 1796*

to learn something about the beauty and culture that surround all of us at Oxford. I suppose I taught myself something about architectural history by measuring old houses and college buildings and about archaeology by digging up their foundations. I learnt by looking as I walked about, and by reading what *I* chose to read, not books on a reading list. I still owe the place a mysterious and intangible debt.

John Ruskin, in later life, wished that his tutors had helped him to use his eyes. Although every detail of the colleges and old houses should be precious to us, Oxford's historic buildings have been cruelly maltreated in recent years and are still gravely at risk from piecemeal alteration. In the interests of cafeteria-service in their dining halls Lincoln College ripped out two fifteenth-century arches in 1957, Merton destroyed two perfect thirteenth-century doorways in 1959, and Trinity knocked out two more ancient arches at about that time. In the 1960s Christ Church destroyed the late-medieval refectory roof of St Frideswide's Priory and the early Tudor roof of Staircase 7, north of Tom Tower. At the same college the Cathedral authorities, advised by the then Cathedral architect, scrubbed off all the medieval wall-paintings that had been revealed in Victorian restorations, except for a group of angels on the Lady Chapel vault. These survive only because of a threatened strike by the Cathedral altarboys, which I organised. Few colleges escaped drastic and unnecessary facelifts in the 1960s and 1970s. Much of Oxford's character has been ruined by ill-advised stone-cleaning, which has caused well-preserved stonework to deteriorate, to be followed by wholesale refacing. There has been scarcely any research on or record of the old stonework. I have never been able to understand why quite so many bursars and architects seem to hate old buildings and long to leave their mark on them. The worst of a generation of poor college extensions was the Blue Boar Quad at Christ Church, designed by the architects Philip Powell and Hidalgo Moya, fashionable for a time in the academic world. Their quad of 1967-8 lacks character and insulation and was always prone to leak and lose its lead cladding. It was fun to meet the architects while they were replanning access to the canons' lodgings on the north side of Tom Quad. To Powell, tall gaunt Dr Leonard Hodgson, Regius Professor of Divinity, was 'Canon Underpass', while his neighbour, the short stooped Dr V.A. Demant, Professor of Moral and Pastoral Theology, was 'Canon Flyover'. To my shame I subscribed £20 towards the quad, before I realised that the college building committee had not given the architects a proper brief and cancelled my next nine years' payments.

Chaotically old-fashioned, Oxford 'this ancient temple of learning' (to quote a recent president of the United States when he came to receive a better degree than the one he flunked) has become an unpleasant place to visit, however fascinating. Cambridge is a more agreeable place to stroll through, although surrounded on three sides by vast science parks on flat farmland, and, to that extent, even more threatened by the skills of the modern world. For the last eight centuries Oxford's main business has been the dreamlike one of selling words with accommodation and food thrown in, and drink too to make it all seem worthwhile. How will the city and university develop? Presenting a timeless face to the innocent onlooker, Oxford seems changeless but is restlessly eager for change. Is the place unable to escape her destiny to continue creating myths and selling words, and will she become ever more intolerable?

BIBLIOGRAPHY

Anthony Wood (1632-95) made an huge contribution to our understanding of Oxford. In his lifetime Wood saw in print only his *Historia et Antiquitates Universitatis Oxoniensis*, 2 vols (1674) and the *Athenae Oxonienses*, 2 vols (1691-2), his biographical study of all Oxford-educated authors. Wood was very unhappy with the *Historia*, much rewritten by John Fell, dean of Christ Church; and he was prosecuted for libel over the latter. In the eighteenth century Sir John Peshall (1718-78) published a version of Wood's *City of Oxford* (1773). John Gutch (1746-1831) edited Wood's *History and Antiquities of the Colleges and Halls* (1790), *Fasti* (1790) and *History of the University* (1792-6). In the nineteenth century Andrew Clark (1856-1922) brought out a more complete *City of Oxford*, 3 vols (1889-99) and edited Wood's diary-notes with extra material as his *Life & Times*, 5 vols (1891-1900). Wood's notes and other sources were listed in Clark's *Life & Times*, vol. 4 (1895). The library of 6,760 pamphlets and printed books that he built up in his rooms in Postmasters Hall in Merton Street survives in the Bodleian Library and has been authoritatively studied by Nicholas Keissling, *The Library of Anthony Wood* (2002).

Since I came to Oxford 65 years ago, 12 big fat books on Oxford have come out:

Royal Commission on Historical Monuments, *City of Oxford* (1939)
Victoria County History of Oxfordshire, vol. 3, *University of Oxford* (1954)
Victoria County History of Oxfordshire, vol. 4, *City of Oxford* (1979)
T. Aston (ed.), *The History of the University of Oxford*, 8 vols (1986-2000)
J. Prest (ed.), *The Illustrated History of Oxford University* (1993)

The first three give us masses of detail in almost unreadable form. The last nine volumes, a vast recent enterprise with many authors, contain 7,500 loosely edited pages, without a comprehensive index. They have some plans and pictures and a few mildly funny stories and no really decent jokes.

Two recent bibliographies list 13,000 books and articles, far more than a lifetime's reading: E.H. Cordeaux & D.H. Merry, *Bibliography of Printed Works relating to the University of Oxford* (1968), with 809 pages and 8,868 items; Cordeaux & Merry, *Bibliography of Printed Works relating to the City of Oxford* (1976), with 391 pages & 3,890 items. Some material on Oxford castle are in the companion *Bibliography on Oxfordshire*.

The Ashmolean Museum, Bodleian Library, Museum of Oxford, Centre for Oxfordshire Studies (at Westgate), Oxfordshire Record Office and Pitt-Rivers Museum, all in Oxford, the British Library and British Museum in London, and the Beinecke Library at Yale together have hundreds of thousands of photographs, drawings, prints of Oxford, of books and papers about the place, many maps and plans, and thousands of things from the city. There are small groups of drawings, etc. in galleries and libraries at Cardiff, Exeter, Ipswich, Liverpool etc.

It is always a pleasure to read lively and unpretentious works such as:
A.J. Arkell, *Oxford Stone* (1947)
Ruth Fasnacht, *A History of the City of Oxford* (1954)
Falconer Madan, *Oxford Outside the Guide-Books* (1923)
Aymer Vallance, *The Old Colleges of Oxford* (1912)

INDEX

ACKNOWLEDGEMENTS

Alun Jones	*16, 69c*
Ashmolean Museum	*9a-b, 27b*
Bodleian Library	*30b, 31, 32a-b, 81b, 86, colour plate 4*
British Library	*35a*
George Lambrick, with Oxford Archaeology & Department for Continuing Education	*3*
Rector and Fellows, Lincoln College, Oxford	*Colour plates 7h, 9c*
Museum of the History of Science, Oxford	*Colour plate 7g*
By kind permission of the Warden and Fellows, New College, Oxford	*Colour plates 7a, 7c, 7d, 9b*
Building Control Services, Oxford City Council	*38b, 39b*
Centre for Oxfordshire Studies, Oxon CC	*Frontispiece*
Oxford University Archives	*65*
By kind permission of the President and Fellows of St John's College, Oxford	*43a-b*
Woodmansterne Publications Limited	*Colour plate 11b*

If you are interested in purchasing other books published by Tempus,
or in case you have difficulty finding any Tempus books in your local bookshop,
you can also place orders directly through our website

www.tempus-publishing.com